GUIDED**PRACTICE**
ROUTINESFOR**GUITAR**
ADVANCED LEVEL

Practice with 128 Guided Exercises in this Comprehensive 10-Week Guitar Course

LEVI**CLAY**

FUNDAMENTAL**CHANGES**

Guided Practice Routines For Guitar – Advanced Level

Practice with 128 Guided Exercises in this Comprehensive 10-Week Guitar Course

ISBN: 978-1-78933-423-4

Published by **www.fundamental-changes.com**

Copyright © 2023 Levi Clay

Edited by Tim Pettingale

www.fundamental-changes.com

Over 12,000 fans on Facebook: **FundamentalChangesInGuitar**

Instagram: **FundamentalChanges**

For over 350 Free Guitar Lessons with Videos Check Out

www.fundamental-changes.com

Cover Image Copyright: Shutterstock, Semisatch

Contents

Introduction

For me, the hardest thing about writing a book has always been the first sentence. Do I go formal? Does "hello" sound odd? Do I assume you know why you're here; that you've read the previous instalments? Or do I act as though this is the first time you're reading my words?

There's no right answer to this conundrum – I just have to take the first step then keep writing. I can always go back and tighten things up later, right?

I'm sure you can see where I'm going with this…

We're here to talk about practice, and practice can sometimes feel like writing a book.

When you practice, you're aiming to document who you are now, while building towards who you want to be in the future. This can feel incredibly daunting – so overwhelming that you might want to give up before you start. That's the first hurdle and probably the biggest, but you have to take a step and commit to the task. You've got to write the first sentence.

The keen eyed among you will have noticed the "advanced" tagline in the title and may already know this book is part of a series. This is the third book in my efforts to tackle the world of practice and help you to make better use of your time.

So, what does *advanced* mean?

The Cambridge dictionary defines it as "modern and well developed", while Merriam-Webster has "far on in time or course". After being a guitarist for 20+ years, it's a word that feels very flexible in its meaning. To be an *advanced* guitarist was something I strived for when I was younger, like a badge of honour. "Oh, he's an *advanced* player!" However, with age comes wisdom and I encourage you to steer away from this idea.

Because the meaning of "advanced" is a bit woolly, it's possible you skipped the foundation and intermediate books in this series, because you consider yourself an advanced player – but it's all relative. I thought I was the cat's pyjamas when I was 15 and could play a bunch of cool sweep picking patterns. In reality, I'd play anything to draw attention away from the fact that if someone mentioned a song, I couldn't play it unless they showed me how. I played a lot of notes, but I didn't *say* a great deal.

Looking back, the only people who thought I was an advanced player were those who couldn't do what I could. In reality, I was a long way off being able to play like Joe Pass or Pat Martino (and still am!) If there's one thing I've learned on my journey, especially from getting to interview many of my childhood heroes, is that the more you learn, the more you realise you need to learn.

So, to enjoy this book, we need to leave our egos at the door. We're not here to prove to ourselves how good we are, we're here to get better. Our aim is to have rock solid control over our instrument and to become a bulletproof musician; someone who, if we're called on to play something, we can instantly do it.

As you've probably gathered, I don't really like the word advanced!!! Instead, let's think about the verb *advance* and what that means. It's about moving forward in a purposeful manner. Forget about being advanced, let's focus on advancing!

Remember that the exercises in this book are *practice routines* rather than *lessons*. In other words, when I sit at the piano to practice scales, I'm not learning them, I'm running through things I already know to build familiarity and find weaknesses that need to be fixed. I'll do my best to explain everything in this book, but some knowledge must be assumed.

For example, it's assumed that you know your major scales in the most important positions, your triad knowledge is pretty good, you understand chord construction, and you can play arpeggios. These are the skills we'll be working on in this book. If you're even slightly dubious about any one of those things, don't be afraid to stop, go back, and work on them via the previous books. It's a cliché, and I use it all the time, but you can't build a house on weak foundations.

For those of you who have worked through my previous couple of books, expect this one to be harder – not just physically harder on the instrument, but on the brain too! These exercises are a little longer than previous ones, so they'll be a good stamina check for you (they are meant to be practiced as complete pieces in their entirety) as well as requiring more thought.

As before, with the help of the audio, you and I will play the routines together. One piece of feedback I received on the first two books was, "It would be better if each exercise had its own audio example" but that would defeat the purpose of the process.

If we did that, this book would be the same as every other guitar book you've read. The point is, you have to *really know* the musical material, so that you can automatically play along with me. This isn't five minutes on the treadmill, it's an assault course! And that will really test whether you've learned the drills or not. That said, I have introduced a bit more space between each exercise in the routines this time, and added clearer count-ins. Use the audio daily and watch your skills progress.

Right, let's get advancing!

Get the Audio

The audio files for this book are available to download for free from **www.fundamental-changes.com.** The link is in the top right-hand corner. Click on the "Guitar" link then simply select this book title from the drop-down menu and follow the instructions to get the audio.

We recommend that you download the files directly to your computer, not to your tablet, and extract them there before adding them to your media library. You can then put them onto your tablet, iPod or burn them to CD. On the download page there are instructions and we also provide technical support via the contact form.

For over 350 free guitar lessons with videos check out:

www.fundamental-changes.com

Over 12,000 fans on Facebook: **FundamentalChangesInGuitar**

Tag us for a share on Instagram: **FundamentalChanges**

Routine One – Major Scale & Filling in the Blanks

When people think of music lessons, often the first thing that comes to mind is scales. We tend to start by learning them, so it's easy to think of scales as something we want to move on from, but they are the foundation on which the language of music is based. Not only are they wonderful for developing fretboard navigation skills, they're awesome for finger dexterity, and there's no better tool to put your picking technique through its paces.

For these exercises, I want you to use nothing but alternate picking. I see a lot of students (of all levels) for whom this is a weakness. To be clear, I'm not talking about *speed* here, just the ability to alternate pick continuously as a subconscious motion. Our picking hand motion should be as automatic as walking or breathing, and I can think of no better way to start a warmup.

In Example 1a, mute all of the strings with the fretting hand. Using a down-up strumming motion, play two bars of 1/16th notes, followed by two bars of playing just the 5th fret of the G string. The motion you use for each should be no different – just a little more controlled and refined for the single notes.

The down beats should always be played with downstrokes, as you would when strumming rhythm guitar chords. This may be a point of frustration for many readers, but if you stick with it, you'll thank me. It will make your rhythm tighter, your picking more controlled, and it'll allow you to focus more on the sound of the notes instead of how you're playing them.

Example 1a:

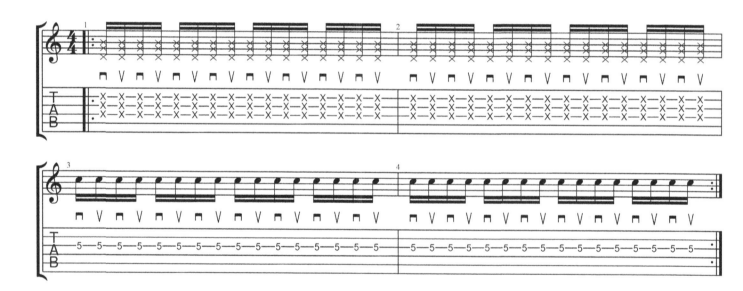

With that reminder out of the way, for the rest of the chapter we'll focus on a decent scale workout!

In the previous two books, I presented all scales in three positions rather than five, so let's review that concept before advancing beyond it.

To make these exercises easier to loop around, we'll start on the root note, ascend to the top of the position, then descend to the bottom of the position, filling out the bar so that we get back to the root when we repeat.

We'll start with a review of the CAGED E shape major scale, played here in the key of G. Play the chord first to remind yourself of the shape that it fits around, then ascend and descend the scale. On the audio, we'll play this routine 8 times.

Example 1b:

Here's the same G Major scale, but now based around a C shape chord.

Example 1c:

Finally, here's the A shape. As before, we're going to cover all six strings here. There's no room for grey areas in our fretboard knowledge!

Example 1d:

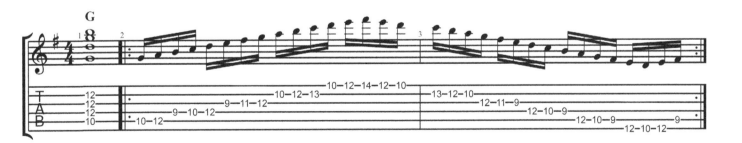

If you've read books 1 and 2, you'll remember the major scale exercise that moved through the Circle of 4ths. We're taking that idea and advancing it here by applying the full, two-octave scale pattern to the chord progression. Yes, this is the first really challenging exercise, both physically and mentally. You'll need some picking stamina for this!

Example 1e:

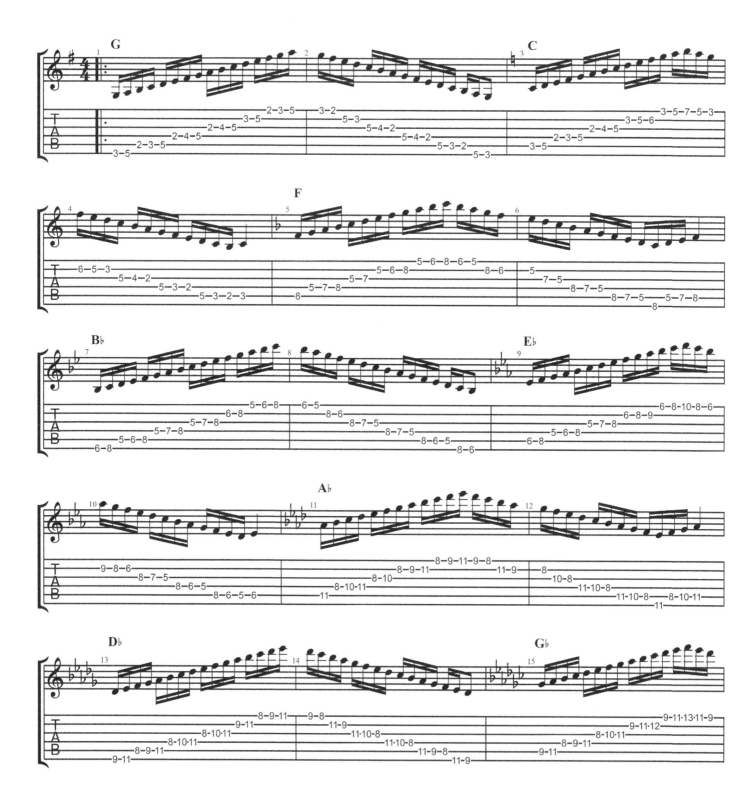

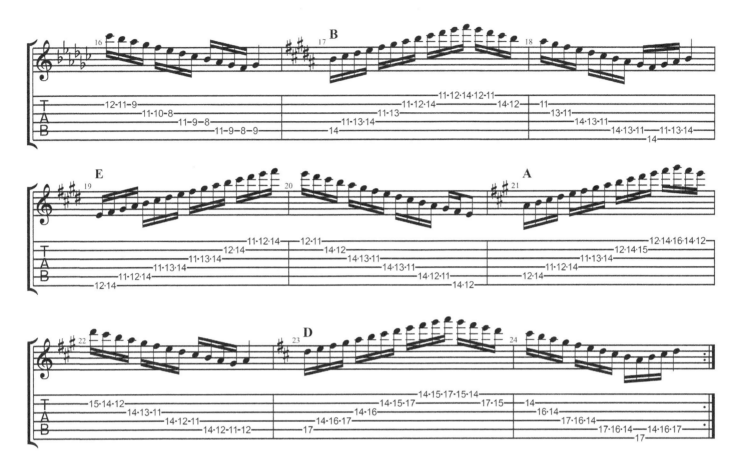

Because we're here to advance our knowledge, and the end goal is to be able to move effortlessly around the neck rather than being stuck in positions, it's worth making sure we know the remaining two positions we've yet to explore, so we have a fuller picture of the fretboard.

First, here is the D shape of the major scale. I almost never play here for the simple reason that I see these notes as crossing over with the E and C shapes. But, when transitioning from one position to another, our hand will probably pass through this shape, so why not *really* know it?

Example 1f:

And lastly, here's the G shape. I often find myself playing in this shape, as it fits around my preferred major pentatonic scale pattern.

Example 1g:

Unless you have giant hands with seven fingers that can span 12 frets, it's impossible to start combining positions without shifting your hand between them. Sometimes we might want to make a feature of this and make the slides audible, but we also need the ability to shift seamlessly between position without the listener hearing it.

The next exercise uses *shift slides* to move between positions. All the notes are picked, but we'll play some notes with the same finger, indicated by a slide symbol in the TAB. We're doing our best to hide the sound of the slides here.

Example 1h is a simple introduction to the idea, using the first three positions of the G Major scale on the top two strings.

Example 1h:

You may have noticed that we avoided slipping into the three-note-per-string system there. Sometimes we're playing two notes on a string, sometimes three. I like to mix things up like this to avoid having my picking falling into the same patterns.

If we adapt this idea to a three-note-per-string fingering pattern, we can play ideas like Example 1i. Notice that the patterns lend themselves well to playing triplets. Although this kind of lick is a little formulaic, it's an important part of any guitarist's vocabulary.

Some players may find four-fret stretches low down on the neck harder to execute, so it's good to have both approaches at your disposal.

Example 1i:

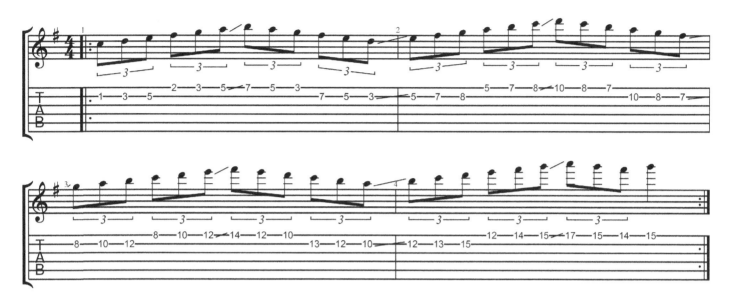

The next slide shift exercise limits us to the D, G, B and high E strings, ascending one position, descending the next, and so on. This limitation exercise forces us to become comfortable with position shifts on the high E and D strings.

Example 1j:

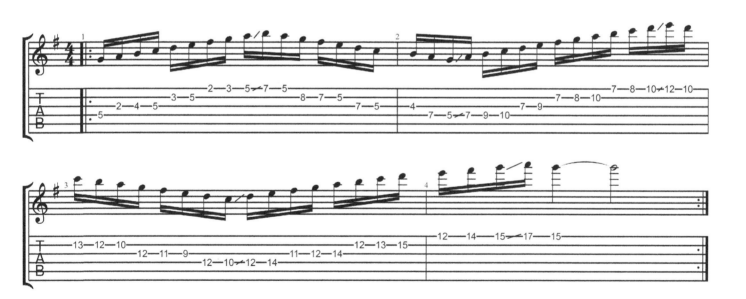

Here's a more challenging slide shift exercise. It feels more random than previous examples because I set out to explore the neck a bit more by sliding in places where I wouldn't normally change position.

Although you can copy what I played here, you should also take the time to find your own pathways through the positions. I don't want you to learn one way, but lots of different ways.

It's like moving house and finding yourself in a new area you're unfamiliar with. The best way to discover the geography is to go for a walk and just explore different directions. It doesn't matter where I am in my town, if you ask me for directions to the post office, I'll get you there!

Example 1k:

We could go on forever with similar exercises because the possibilities are endless when it comes to transition points between positions. Ultimately, your goal is to be confident shifting from position to position at any point in the scale, not just at the top or bottom.

Take some time to test yourself with this ear training exercise. I can't write this out for you, otherwise you won't have anything to work out!

- Play any scale position from the bottom, ascend two strings and stop at the highest scale note on that string

- Now *sing* the next note in the scale. Really focus on *hearing* that note in relation to your current position. Is it located on the same string, or the next one? Is it one fret higher or two? (These are the only two options)

- Reverse it and play a scale position from the top, descending two strings and stopping on the lowest note on that string.

- Sing the next note

Initially, something like this might seem very hard to do, but the more you do it, the more automatic it becomes, until you can do it without thinking. You'll find that this exercise has the massive benefit of helping you to change positions without any real thought. You'll just follow your ear to make the transition you need.

In the next exercise I want to challenge you with some consecutive slides. In the heat of the battle, when we're taking a solo on a gig, there's not much time to think and we're not always going to make smart fingering choices. At this moment, it's good to have the technique to recover, rather than stop and say, "Oh no, I used the wrong finger there, I need to start over!"

Being able to make smooth transitions like this will elevate your control of the instrument, but it will also open up different fingering patterns and phrasing ideas. Play the first two notes of each phrase with the first and second fingers and use the third finger for the slides.

Example 1l:

It's good to test how we might play something without the optimal finger dexterity we're used to. Here's a G Major scale but you must play it without using your little finger. That means either stretching further than normal with the third finger or using careful shift slides to hide the issues. Get this sounding as seamless as possible.

Example 1m:

Let's try that again but now only using the first two fingers.

Example 1n:

And, finally, a scale played with just one finger!

I know what you're thinking, why would I ever need to do that? The answer is, you probably won't unless you play a lot of slide guitar, like me. But the point of this exercise is to test how good your visualisation is of scale positions.

It's easy to learn a scale pattern, then switch off and allow muscle memory to do all the work. Playing a one-fingered scale means we *have to know* what notes are in the scale, recognise the intervals, and have a pretty solid shift slide technique to make it happen.

Example 1o:

To say we're only scratching the surface here would be a mild understatement, but I want to get onto other things, and I don't want you to have a 15-hour routine! Who know, maybe there will be a *Guided Practice Routines for Guitar – Scale Workouts* in the future?!

Get to work and I'll see you in a week!

Routine Two – Four Triad Types

Last week we took a deep dive into scales. Scales are linear by nature, like a shopping list you might take to the supermarket. You've got your eggs, milk, bread, bacon, coffee, jam, toothpaste, detergent, steak, pasta, cheese, etc. I'm sure you can weave a story in your mind of how you might use those items during a week.

A triad/chord is like a snapshot of the list. It can be hard to decipher a long list, but if I said to you, "Bacon, eggs and bread", you immediately know those things work together to make a tasty snack. "Milk, jam and toothpaste", not so much!

This analogy helps me when thinking about chords. A chord is a vertical visualisation of part of a scale. It shows how things can work together, rather than picking random ingredients and hoping for the best. (Though by all means throw some toothpaste on your steak if that's the kind of dissonant flavour you're looking for! Music is amazing – you can be that mad scientist if you want!)

In this chapter we're going to review major and minor triads in all their closed voice positions, and we'll also look at how to create their augmented and diminished cousins. Together, these are the building blocks of all western harmony, and mastery of them will create a network of harmonic skeletons you can use to create literally any chord, scale or sound you desire.

We'll start with the major triad.

From the root note of the G Major scale, we play the 1st, 3rd and 5th degrees of the scale. This gives us the notes G, B and D.

When we think about the major triad, it's good to recognise the intervals of each note relative to the root.

B is four semitones or a major 3rd from G.

D is seven semitones or a perfect 5th from G.

The major triad will always have the formula 1, 3, 5.

If we take the G major triad and map the notes across the fretboard, we immediately see three obvious positions in which to play it across the strings – which is the reason why I always tend to think in a three-position system.

For example, starting on the low E string, 3rd fret, we can play the G major triad in three-note groupings on adjacent strings, moving across the neck, without changing position. Each three-note grouping will contain the notes G, B and D, and doing this produces *four*, three-note voicings.

Sometimes the order of notes will be G, B, D, sometimes B, D, G, and sometimes D, G, B, but they will always be the ingredients of a G major triad.

Some people might call these inversions, but I don't think of them or hear them that way. An inversion is where a note other than the root is played in the bass, but when I play these voicings, I hear a low G under them all. You'll get this as soon as you play the exercise.

We'll start our routine by playing the four little triad voicings in each of the three positions. We'll descend through all four patterns in the E shape, then all four patterns in the C shape, and finally all four patterns in the A shape. In the fourth bar we'll repeat the C shape patterns.

To keep us on our toes, after we've played the G major triad this way, we'll repeat the exercise for D and C major triads.

For the D major triad, we're beginning in the C shape, then moving up to the A and E.

For the C major triad, we're beginning in the A shape, then moving up to the E, then C.

Example 2a:

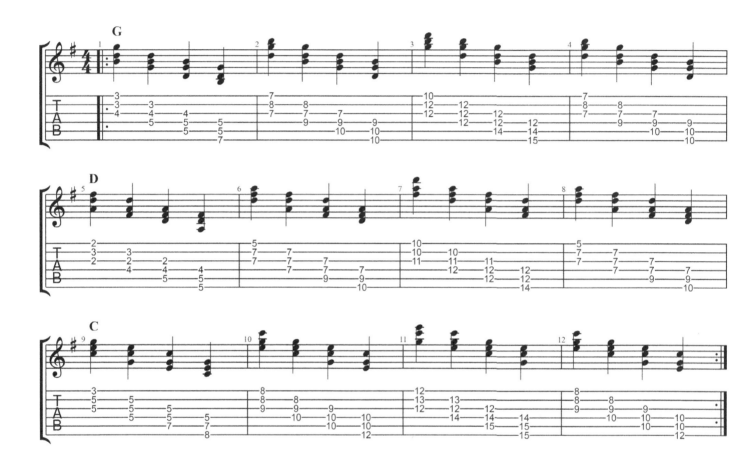

These triads we're a game changer for me – they really helped to establish the three positions I've come to base all my playing on. I first got this from Mick Goodrick's classic work (coincidently titled) *The Advancing Guitarist*.

Prior to that, I would only ever practice triads along a string, and that always felt harder, as I was constantly having to visualise a new shape. That doesn't mean it's not worth practicing though. If anything, this next exercise is just as important as the last. Both help develop our visualisation in different directions. The last example was vertical, this one is horizontal.

Here are G, D and C major triad voicings again, but now moving along the neck on each string set.

Example 2b:

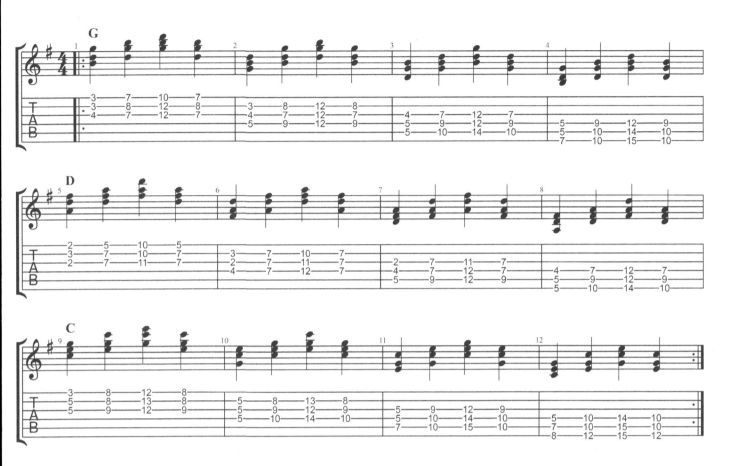

When we start to think about *minor* triads, we realise that learning where the 3rd of each of these voicings is located is incredibly important. If we take the G major triad and lower the 3rd (B) by a semitone, we get a b3 (Bb) and now we have the ingredients of a G minor triad: G, Bb, D.

Although I know all my minor triad shapes as patterns in their own right, when I was first learning them, it was valuable to see how minor voicings could be created from major voicings. This helps to teach us where the b3 note lives around each of the three main positions – and this in turn helps us when forming chords or playing melodies.

I can't stress this enough: when I play any triad, I always see it in relation to a root note on the low E, A, or D string. Doing this significantly cuts down the amount of work the brain has to do.

To illustrate this, here's a great visualisation exercise that moves between major and minor triads, played using the G, D and C shapes of G major/minor.

Example 2c:

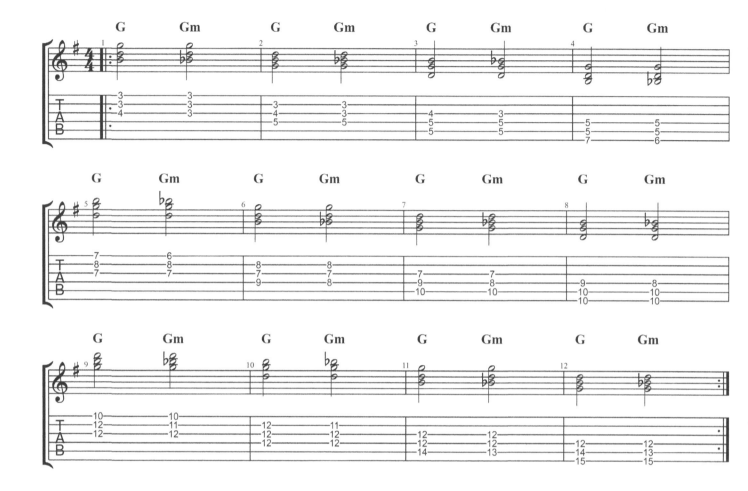

Next, we move onto diminished and augmented triads, starting with the diminished.

The diminished triad occurs naturally in the major scale and is found on the 7th degree. In G Major, that's an F# note.

Starting on F# and stacking the notes in 3rds we get F#, A, C.

As before, we'll visualise the intervals in relation to the root of the chord.

F# to A is a minor 3rd.

F# to C is a b5.

So, a diminished triad has the formula 1 b3 b5. In other words, it's like a minor triad where the 5th is flattened.

I'm sure you can see where we're going with this! Just as we can use a major triad as a visual reference to create a minor triad, we can use our minor triad knowledge to form diminished triads by flattening the 5th.

That's what this next exercise does. We're using the G, D and C shapes again, but this time I'm mixing things up by moving horizontally along the fretboard, rather than vertically. We gotta keep you on your toes!

Example 2d:

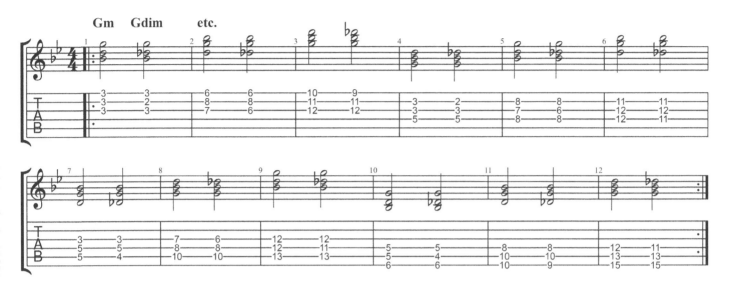

The final primary colour of triad is the augmented. This triad doesn't occur naturally in the major scale like the others, but when you start getting into more exotic sounds like the melodic minor or whole tone scale, it will come up all the time. I love this sound!

When you think about it, to "diminish" means to make something smaller, and in the diminished triad we're making the distance from the 5th to the root smaller by flattening it. To "augment" means to make something greater and in the augmented triad we're making the distance from the 5th to the root bigger by sharpening it.

So, the augmented triad has the formula 1 3 #5 and a G augmented triad has the notes G, B, D#.

The guitar is an inherently shape-based instrument. I'm using note names because it's always good to know what the actual notes are, but when I'm *playing*, I'm not thinking, "OK, the notes of G augmented are… and the notes of C augmented are…" because the *shape* of those chords is the same.

Remember, if you can see a root note, you can see a position, and therefore you can see a chord.

Many readers will know I also play piano. Here, it's the opposite: I can't rely on shapes because the piano is a linear instrument. I need to know the pitches in a chord or scale. But shapes work wonderfully on guitar, so why not use that to our advantage?

You'll have noticed that a G augmented triad is just a G major triad with a #5, so in this exercise we play those triads in turn.

Also notice the wonderful symmetry in the augmented shapes. All three notes are a major 3rd apart, and this means we can move them around the fretboard in major 3rds. Gaug, Baug and D#aug all contain the same notes. Fascinating stuff!

Example 2e:

I've always found that the best way to practice triads is with chord scales using common progressions. Here is every triad in the key of G Major:

Gmaj – Am – Bm – Cmaj – Dmaj – Em – F#dim

Chords I, IV and V are major, chords ii, iii and vi are minor, and chord vii is diminished.

This pattern remains the same, regardless of the key signature. So, for example, in the key of E Major (E, F#, G#, A, B, C#, D#) the triads are:

Emaj – F#m – G#m – Amaj – Bmaj – C#m – D#dim

Example 2f illustrates a G Major chord-scale, using just the E shape triad on the D, G and B strings. Play this a few times and you'll see the pattern of intervals between the shapes.

I.e., there is a tone between chord I (G) and chord ii (Am), a tone between chord ii and chord iii (Bm), and a semitone between Bm and chord IV (Cmaj), etc.

This is a fabulous way to develop the skill of finding major and minor triads without overloading yourself. As you're only using one shape, you can focus on seeing the slight difference between major and minor (and eventually diminished) shapes.

Example 2f:

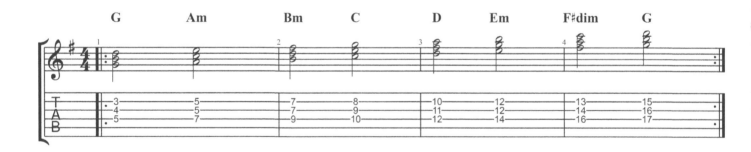

The next example uses the same idea applied to the G, B and high E strings. When I play this, I'm visualising the root note for each chord on the low E string. So, this exercise doesn't feel any more challenging than the previous one – I see them as both rooted on the low E.

Example 2g:

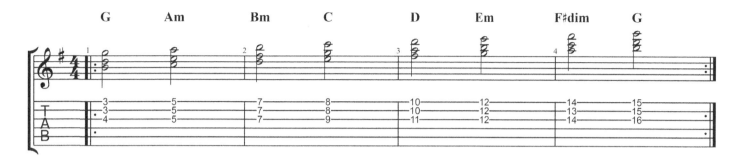

Now let's repeat the exercise but in the key of D. We won't stop to consider the notes in that key, we'll just focus on knowing our major, minor and diminished triad shapes, and the intervallic distance between each chord as we move up the neck.

Start with the major triad on the G, B and high E string set at the 2nd fret. Move up a tone to the next chord, which will be minor. Can you immediately see what the minor triad should look like? If not, why not? Finding the weaknesses in your skills then going back to develop them is what it means to advance on your instrument. Sometimes you need to go back to go forward!

Example 2h:

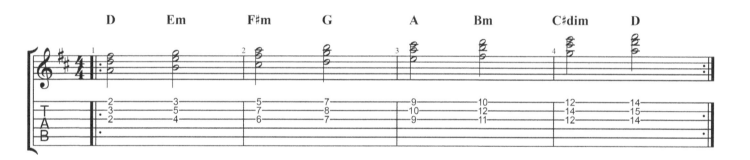

How about doing that in C, using the A, D, G string set in the CAGED A shape?

I could easily fill a book with these chordal exercises (maybe I will soon!), but we're not looking to make our own version of George Van Eps' *Harmonic Mechanisms for Guitar* or Ted Greene's *Chord Chemistry* – this is about creating a practice routine.

So, you're free to play exactly what I've written here, but think about the knowledge you've gained. You now know 12 major triad voicings, and that means there are 12 different chord scales you could play on your guitar. A healthy practice regime will mix those up at random, so that you're always on your toes but becoming more and more confident each time you try it.

Example 2i:

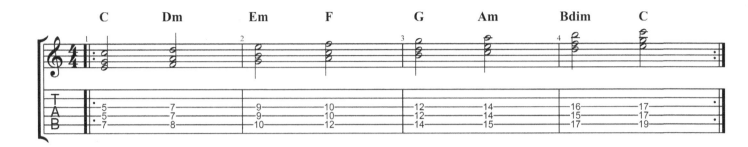

To take this exercise to the next level, we can mix triad voicings to stay as close to one position as possible. This will require more thought than just ascending a familiar pattern.

For example, say we're in the third fret area playing a G major triad on the D, G, B strings, and we want to move to A minor. We can move up using the same shape and alter the triad to make it minor. Or we can play A minor down in the open position. This immediately breaks us out of the previous rut.

Next, we want to play B minor. For this we could just move two frets higher. Then it's C major. For that, we can use the CAGED A shape again and barre at the 5th fret.

Next, D major. Rather than move up two frets and copy the previous shape, why not play it using the C shape below? Then move back up again for the E minor… and so on.

All this requires more thought than following a pattern, but we're here to get serious right?

Check out the following example that illustrates this approach. The voicings are chosen so that we're always working in the same zone of the neck.

Example 2j:

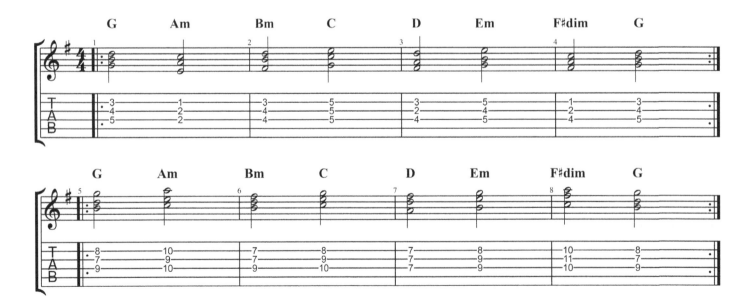

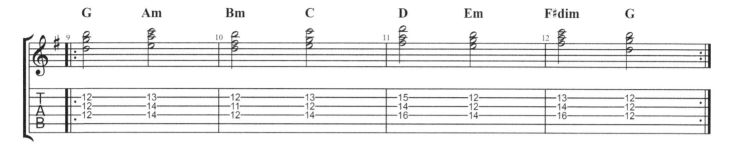

Let's pause for a moment.

The previous exercise used just one string set, but you bet I can do that on any string set you ask *and* I'm likely to mix them up and play different ones each time I practice.

Of course, that has required a lot of working out, but working things out is the best practice we can possibly do. Don't rely on someone feeding you the answers – know how to find the solution to the problem yourself and you'll be unstoppable.

Now for the final exercises in this routine where we apply our triad knowledge to real-world chord progressions.

Here's one that uses both major and minor triads and also includes a chord not in the key of G. Get this sort of thing under your fingers and you'll be free as a bird when it comes to playing rhythm guitar or making melodies.

Example 2k:

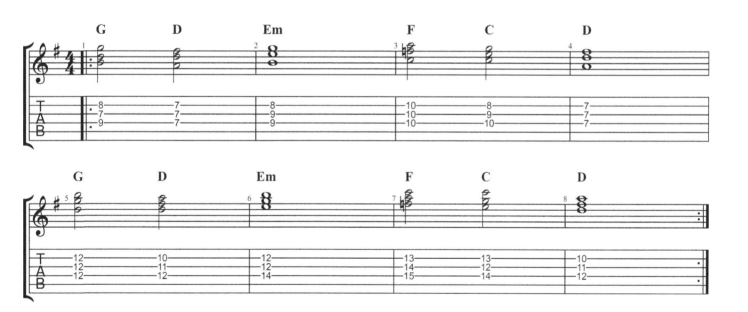

And lastly, a different progression, still using a mixture of major and minor triads. This will feel hard at first, but don't worry, *you will survive!*

Example 21:

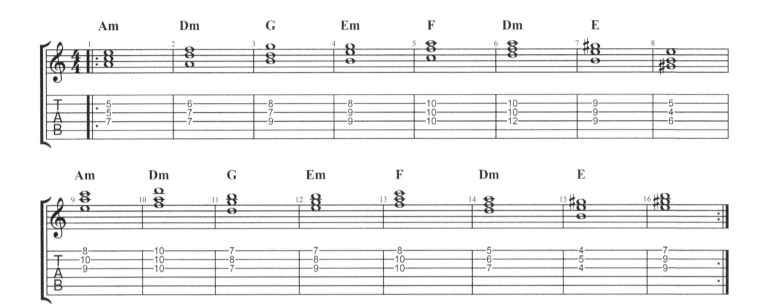

Now get to work, and I'll see you in a week.

Routine Three – Advanced 1/16 Note Rhythms

While I might downplay the importance of pitch recognition to my students, due to the shape-based nature of our instrument and the wide availability of TAB for guitar players, the same can't be said for rhythm.

In my work as a transcriber, people often ask me if I have perfect pitch. The answer is no, but also why would I need it? If I hear a note, while it might be lovely to immediately identify it as a Db, I can quickly find it on the guitar through trial and error. And the more often I do that, the more often my initial guess is correct.

It's easy to develop pitch recognition over time, but rhythmic comprehension is an altogether more complex beast. Rhythm is how we place events over a defined period of time. We don't just hear a song as one long piece of sound, we pay attention to the little markers that tell us what's going on and we perceive its pulse. I say *perceive*, because the pulse isn't a tangible thing in music, it's just something we agree on. So, understanding rhythm requires a) an awareness of the passage of time and b) where musical events occur in relation to a collective hallucination called a pulse. Pretty wild when you think about it, right?!

The question is, how will it help us advance as guitarists?

We can get so far without understanding music in its written form. We can listen to and imitate what we hear, and that takes some people as far as they ever need to go. But there are two skills that will remain closed off to us if we take this route.

The first is transcription. If you can't hear a rhythm and write it down, then you can't write down the music you listen to and love. This extends to composing your own music and writing out arrangements to play with other musicians. I play in a soul band where I act as musical director to seven other musicians, plus anyone who might sit in with us on a gig. While I can explain the rhythmic ending of a song, or spell out a bassline by vocalising it, and hope the musician understands me, it's helpful for everyone if I can write it down.

The second is the ability to study more complicated music in greater detail. Imagine learning a simple three-chord song but not knowing the names of the chords. If you know what the chords are, then it takes less brain power to play, right? It saves you from having to learn some arbitrary way of placing your fingers on the strings. To my mind, rhythm is the same. If I imagine a complex rhythm, the ability to visualise that idea clearly in my mind makes it much easier to memorise long passages of music in detail.

The previous two books in this series both had chapters on rhythm, so today we're jumping right into some complex 1/16th note syncopations and ties.

Let's warm up by alternate picking some 1/16th notes. This might seem basic, but we're getting the picking hand motion in place that will keep us true as the examples get more complicated.

No matter what happens, your hand should always be moving down-up-down-up and hitting the notes you need. This will allow you to keep rock solid time and not think too much about having to count or think where the notes fall. In time, your picking hand will just take care of things.

Example 3a:

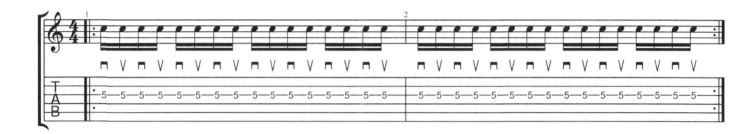

Let's look more closely at how the picking hand motion is amazing at keeping time.

In bar one of the following exercise, we play constant 1/16th notes for the first three beats, then leave beat 4 empty. However, we keep the picking hand moving down and up, so that we're perfectly placed to come back in on beat 1 of the next bar.

In bar two, we'll play 1/16th notes on beats 1 and 3 but leave beats 2 and 4 empty. Again, the motion in the picking hand will keep us solid, so keep it moving!

Now the real challenge. We're going to play beat 1 of bar three, then nothing for the remainder of that bar and bar four. This is a real test of our awareness of time and feel, but the easiest way to ensure we come back in at the right place is to keep that hand moving.

On the audio I play through this exercise four times. The first two times I keep the metronome click going during the silence, but for the subsequent two I remove it. This means you'll need to do your own timekeeping, and it's a very straightforward way of testing how good that is. I learned the "disappearing metronome" approach from Victor Wooten and still use it to make sure my time is good. One tip is to make use of your body's motion and sense of the pulse to keep things tight.

Example 3b:

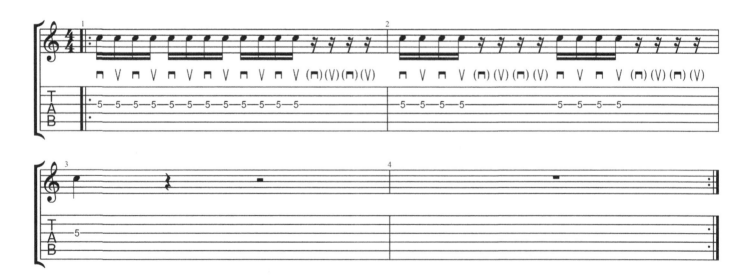

Let's quickly review the four key 1/16th note rhythms from the previous book. These are rhythms you should already know well. Remember that the focus here is not just switching off and playing the rhythms. Instead, focus on actually *reading them* as you play them. Our aim here is to strengthen the connection between what we see, what we hear, and what our body needs to do to create that sound. Here are the rhythms:

1. Four straight 1/16th notes

2. The gallop (an 1/8th note, then two 1/16th notes played down-down-up)

3. The reverse gallop (two 1/16th notes, then an 1/8th note played down-up-down)

4. The syncopated pattern of 1/16th note, 1/8th note, 1/16th note, played down-up-up.

Think of these rhythms like four different words that you need to learn to read in a book.

Example 3c:

Here's a longer example that mixes those rhythms together. Don't forget, your goal is not to memorise the rhythms, it's to develop the skill to read them when presented with them. This might feel intimidating but think of it as combining four words you already know. Use the picking hand motion to keep time and ensure each note is placed correctly.

Example 3d:

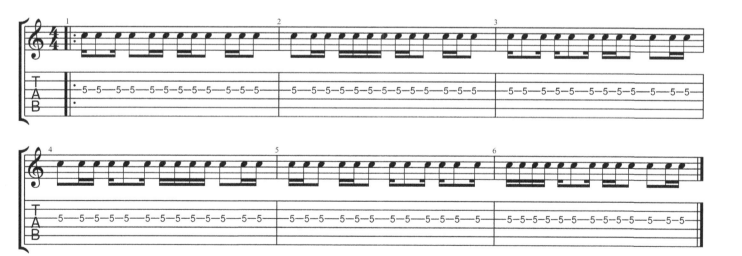

Now let's talk about ties. So far, we've only used four different rhythmic phrases, but this number goes up exponentially when we start using ties to connect two notes. Before playing an exercise, let's get some theory out of the way.

Below is a written example with no TAB. In bar one we play a gallop followed by a reverse gallop. Instead of playing these rhythms like two separate words, we can use a tie to connect them. In bar two, the last 1/16th note in beat 1 is connected to the first 1/16th note in beat 2. That note is now tied across the end of the first beat and the beginning of the second.

Bar three uses the same rhythm but instead of a tie I've used an 1/8th note. This is bad writing and shows that we're just using trial and error to write notation without really understanding it. Why? Because when we look at this rhythm we don't see any words we're familiar with. We can't break it down and if you asked me where beat 2 begins, I'd have to say it's halfway through one of those 1/8th notes. This makes reading the rhythm more difficult than it needs to be.

The goal of writing down a rhythm is to make the task of reading it as easy as possible for other musicians.

Here's a longer example for you to practice reading. Before you dive in with your instrument, take a glance over it. You should be able to see that it's a combination of rhythms you're already comfortable with. I've included picking directions for the first half as guidance. Notice the ties and remember that every time we tie into a new beat, we keep the picking hand moving. The motion should still be there, but we're not hitting the string. My students have always found it tricky not to hit the string with a downstroke, but it's the best way to master time and rhythm.

Example 3e:

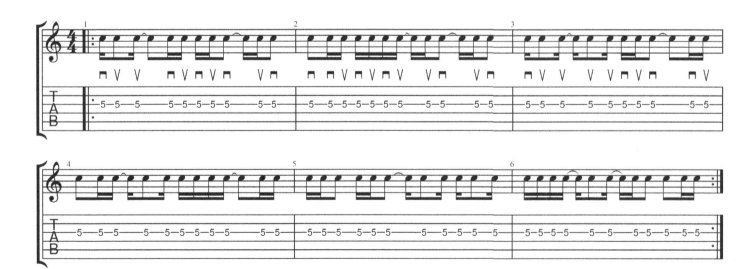

All the rhythms in the previous example were syncopated but I limited them to syncopations between beats in a bar. However, we can also tie notes across bars, meaning that we skip the downbeat on beat 1 too! These rhythms are also common and should be practiced.

The value in an exercise like this is both technical and academic. Before playing it, take some time to try and understand it. Look through it and see if it makes sense to you. If there are areas that don't make sense, break them down *before* relying on your ears to copy what you hear.

Example 3f:

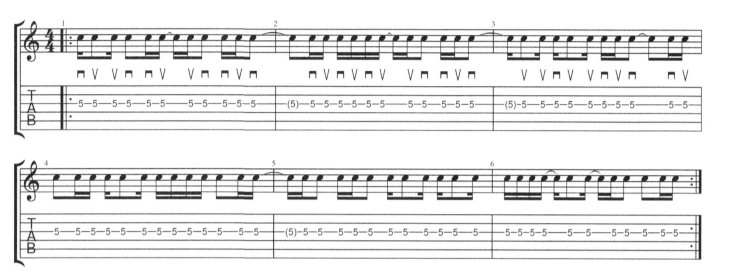

We'll come back to some of these rhythms in the examples at the end of the chapter. I encourage you to pick up a few TAB books and look through them for these rhythms. I used to sit and read books while the music was playing to help build the connection between the sounds I was hearing and how they looked on the page.

The beautiful thing about developing a skill like rhythm reading is that every problem you come across is solvable. It's not like creative writing where opinion comes in. As long as you have enough understanding of how rhythm works, you can figure out how to play anything if you're methodical about it.

Here's another longer reading example. This time we'll use syncopated rhythms with ties *and* rests. 1/16th and 1/8th note rests can look confusing at first, but remember the goal is to clearly see each beat. It all comes back to those beat-long phrases that I hope you've put plenty of practice into.

Example 3g:

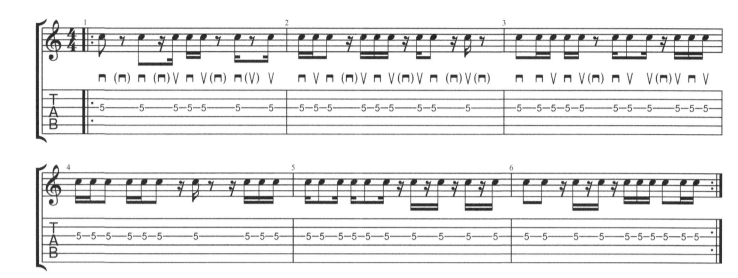

Now let's quickly touch on two more rhythmic "words". This time we're using dotted 1/8th notes. I hate the technical definition of a dotted note! A dotted note takes the value of the original note then adds half its length again. Yuk, sounds too much like an equation to me!

I like to look at the phrase that takes up beat 1 and break it down. Look at the end of the phrase and you can see that it's a 1/16th note. So, surely the note before it must take up the rest of that space? We can use that information to deduce that the first note in the phrase is the length of three 1/16th notes combined. Or, we could say that you play the first note in the beat then hit the final 1/16th note. To me, that's the simplest way and it's bulletproof! The opposite of this would be a 1/16th note followed by a dotted 1/8th. Can you piece that together?

Example 3h:

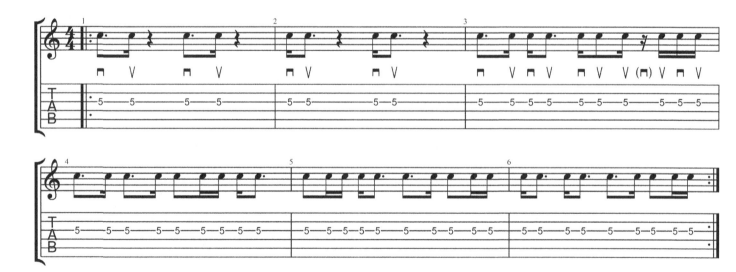

We'll end this routine with some real-life musical examples. This will be a test of your rhythm reading skills. Study the written rhythms and see if you can break them down and understand them.

Example 3i:

Example 3j:

Example 3k:

I could devote an entire book to this, because rhythm is a deep subject, but if you've followed what we've done so far, you'll have developed some advanced skills that will prepare you for most professional musical settings.

Go to work and I'll see you in a week!

Routine Four – Triads & Major Scales

When I sat down to sketch out the outline for this book, I knew this was going to be my favourite chapter. It was working on these exercises that really helped me to glue together some pieces of information for myself.

Anyone who has followed my work will know that I reference triads all the time. They form the foundation of my visualisation on the instrument, so that when I play, everything is just embellished triads in my mind.

Sometimes I get asked about this because people can't see/hear the connection. Instead, they're hearing scales, pentatonic phrases, and chromatic stuff. But though I rarely play just the notes of a triad, they underpin everything. Without them, I couldn't play my musical ideas all over the neck.

In routines one and two we reviewed the major scale, then triads. Skip back and revisit those if you need to, but in this chapter we're going to work on building scales around each triad voicing as a way of preventing us seeing scales as linear entities that go from the lowest to highest note in a given position. Instead, we're going to view them as the flesh on our chordal skeletons.

I always explain to my students that my method of teaching (and learning) is "If this, therefore this".

In other words, if we don't know something, we deduce it from other things we *do* know.

To cite a simple example: if we know the note F is a semitone higher than E, and we know that the low string of the guitar is an E, then the first fret must be an F note. *If this, therefore this.*

I want you to take on board this mentality throughout this chapter, rather than trying to brute force scale shapes into your brain. I'll show you what I mean…

The first exercise here goes back to the G major triad arranged on the D, G and B strings.

Let's pause and consider the intervals in this triad.

The lowest note is the root on the D string, while the 3rd is located on the G string, and the 5th on the B string.

If we want to play the major scale around this triad, after playing the G root on the D string, the next note in the scale is the major 2nd. We can either *know* where this note is or know how to *find* it.

If you immediately know it, great, but if not, what *do* we know?

We know that the note on the G string is the 3rd of the chord. If that note is the 3rd, where is the 2nd? It can't be one fret lower, that's the b3 of the minor triad. So, it must be two frets lower. *If this, therefore this.* It's the A note on the 2nd fret.

Next, we play the 3rd, which we already know, then comes the 4th degree of the scale. Where is it located? Rather than trying to count up the scale from the root, we should know that the 4th is one fret higher than the 3rd, so we play the C note at the 5th fret.

We can continue this logic until we've worked out all the notes of the major scale mapped around the triad.

To get us warmed up, let's play the triad, ascend and descend part of the major scale, then play the triad again.

Example 4a:

As you know from our previous studies, the triad form in the previous example is just one fragment of a larger form in 3rd position. So, to get a glimpse of the full potential of this idea, I'm going to flesh out the whole position and play the G major triad on each string set.

Starting from the *highest* note in each form, we'll play a melodic line using the G Major scale, and each line will end on the *lowest* note in the triad.

This is a great way of advancing your thinking by diving into the scale at various points, plus each idea is rooted in a triad form.

Example 4b:

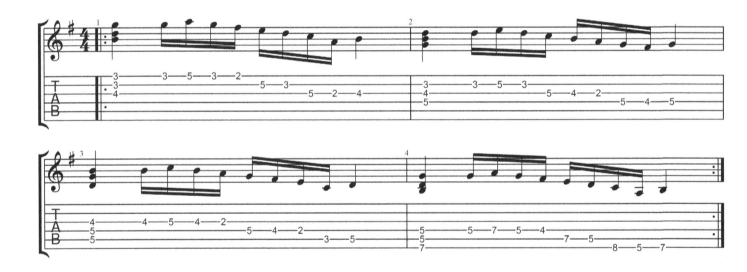

The next example does the same thing based around the C shape of G major. When playing this, engage your ears. Look at your instrument, see the notes you're going to play, and use your "inner ear" to anticipate what the next note will sound like.

This is practical ear training and infinitely more valuable than the classic "Here are two notes... what interval is that?"

We all want to get to the place where we can play anything we hear in our head; where our hands just know what to do. This is how we work on that!

Example 4c:

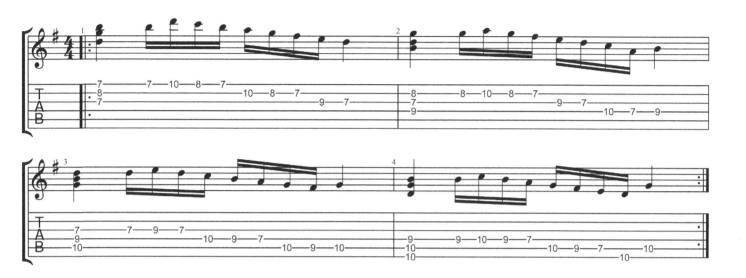

Let's do that again, this time using the A shape of G major. I'll keep making the point – we're not doing this by memorising scale shapes, we need to be able to do it on the fly by looking for what we need to play. The more we focus on this, the easier it becomes to stop looking and rely on our ears.

Example 4d:

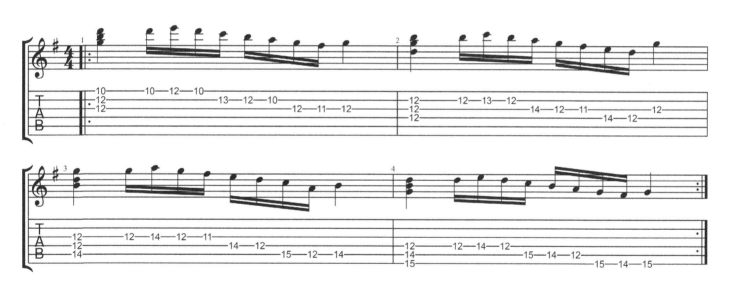

So far, we've covered the major scale relentlessly, but I don't use it too much in my playing as a blues/soul guitarist. In my world, the Mixolydian (or Dominant scale as I prefer to call it) is much more useful, so let's do the exact same exercise, this time with the Dominant scale.

If you need to learn this scale, you may have skipped the previous books in this series, so go and fix that! In short, the Mixolydian/Dominant scale is a major scale with a b7, and it fits perfectly over dominant 7 chords.

As this process starts to come together for you, this bit of information should be all you need. In the major scale, the 7th is always located one fret below the root note, so therefore the b7 is going to be two frets below the root, or alternatively, one fret above the 6th.

In the next exercise the triad has changed to G7 and we're playing the Dominant scale around each form instead of the major scale. Listen to how that sounds and get familiar with the intervals.

Example 4e:

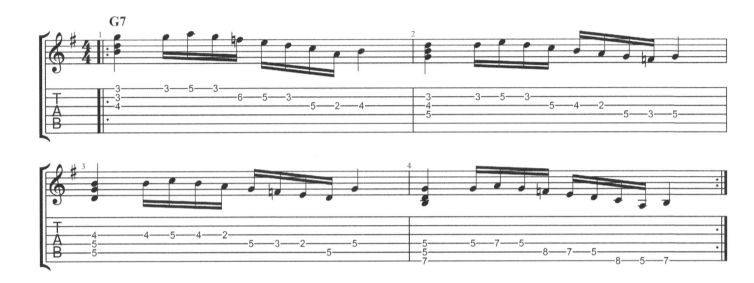

Next, here are both the C and A shapes of G7 presented as one long exercise. This might feel like you have 100 new things to learn, but actually it's only one thing. You've already done it for the major scale, so all you need to know is, *where is that b7?*

Example 4f:

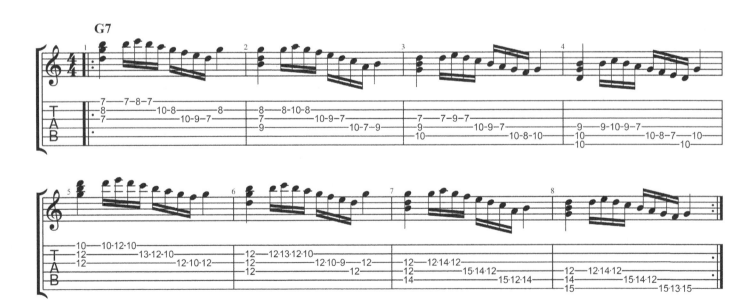

We can repeat this process for other triad forms and their associated scales.

So far, we've looked at:

Major scale: formula 1 2 3 4 5 6 7

Dominant scale: formula 1 2 3 4 5 6 b7

In the final chapter of book 2 in this series we began drilling the Dorian mode. What is that?

Dorian mode: formula 1 2 b3 4 5 6 b7

Notice that the Dorian is hardly any different from the Mixolydian. It just has a b3 to differentiate it, and it fits perfectly over a minor chord. Let's explore it in the same way we've been doing.

Example 4g:

I won't bore you by doing this all over the neck. You know the principle by now. You can practice your triad shapes across all positions, then practice fitting the relevant scale around each one. This is something you might want to mix into your practice routines to keep you on your toes.

Before moving on, I want to show you how this knowledge really changed my life as a player.

As a teenager I was always at bursting point, trying to memorise hundreds of chords, scales and arpeggios in different keys all over the neck, and it was all too much. When I got to music school, the teachers would test us by saying things like, "Play mode 5 of the harmonic minor scale in the A shape." (I know, sounds hellish, right?) It became apparent that they were just testing who had the best memory, not who had the most useful knowledge.

As it happens, mode 5 of the harmonic minor scale is used quite regularly, but at the time it was just a set of three-note-per-string patterns to me. I had no real understanding of it.

This mode is called the Phrygian Dominant. A phrygian scale is normally minor, but this one has a major rather than a minor 3rd and fits over a dominant chord.

Phrygian Dominant has the formula: 1 b2 3 4 5 b6 b7

If we try to think about this as a scale pattern mapped over the fretboard, that's overwhelming, but what about our method? *If this, therefore this.*

If we root this sound with triad shapes, then focus on playing the intervals of the scale around it, suddenly the task of mastering this sound becomes massively easier.

When I first did this, I found that suddenly I could play this sound without really hesitating, and I could do so anywhere on the neck.

Not only that, but my lines were so connected to my triads that they couldn't help but sound like the chord. This was my eureka moment.

Example 4h:

OK, we've looked at how we can use our triad knowledge to build scale patterns around those voicings, so that we can play scale-based ideas anywhere on the neck. How else can we use this knowledge?

How about moving horizontally along the neck, using scale tones to connect different positions? You may not have thought about this being an interesting way to connect your chord positions with melody. Play through this exercise.

Example 4i:

The beauty of this exercise is that you can apply it on any string set.

Example 4j:

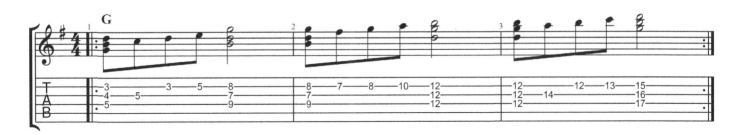

You can also change the melody note to be in the middle of a triad.

Example 4k:

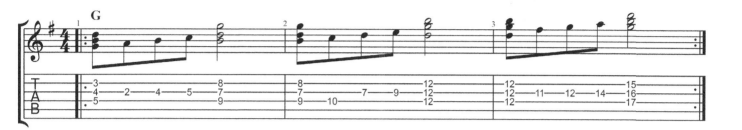

Or you can play the melody from the bottom note of the triad.

Example 4l:

I'm sure you can see the potential of this idea that we've really only scratched the surface of here. We can apply it to minor and dominant triads too. With practice, the only limit will be your imagination. If you put in the work to break down those walls, you'll be able to create anything.

Where can this idea lead?

Ultimately, it can help you play over chord changes like never before.

To end, here's a little etude in C Major that rolls around the progression Dm7 – G7b9 – C6 – A7b9, mixing and matching triad shapes and connecting each chord with some melody. (See Example 4h for a reminder of the Phrygian Dominant sound!)

The more work you put into knowing your triads across the neck, the more effortless something like this will become.

Example 4m:

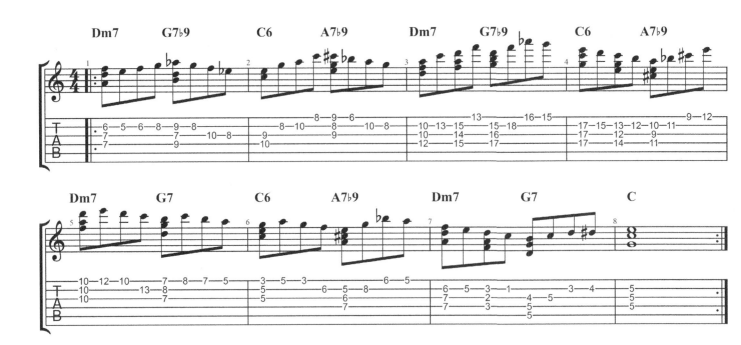

I hope you've enjoyed learning this chapter as much as I have writing it. Get to work and I'll see you in a week!

Routine Five – Triads To 7th Chords

Last week we worked on developing the relationship between chords and scales. The better we get at recognising and locating intervals, the more we tend to see chords and scales as the same thing. A chord is just a vertical snapshot of a sound, versus the scale's linear view of the same sound.

This week, building on our triad work, we're going to consider 7th chords and look at how we can use our triad knowledge as a tool to play them.

First, let's define a 7th chord.

We created triads by stacking notes in 3rds. Three notes make a triad, and if we add one more 3rd interval, we have a 7th chord.

A triad's formula is 1 3 5

A 7th chord's formula is 1 3 5 7

In the key of G Major, if we stack 3rds to create a series of 7th chords we get:

Gmaj7 – Am7 – Bm7 – Cmaj7 – D7 – Em7 – F#m7b5

Now, while technically a 7th chord has four notes, that doesn't mean we *have to* play all four notes to make the sound of a 7th chord.

In my previous book we focused on guide tone voicings – chords that contain just the root, 3rd and 7th. These are the crucial tones that tell us what type of chord we're dealing with. Although the 5th can serve to thicken up the sound of a chord, most of the time it's not particularly important in defining the sound and can be left out.

In this chapter, we're going to learn that even the root note isn't that important. I know, that sounds wild! But in most practical, musical situations, you'll often be playing with a bass player or keyboard player. With these instruments establishing the root notes, we can afford to leave them out. And even if we don't work with other musicians, the human brain is really good at establishing musical context and filling in the blanks.

So, this is my approach to creating 7th chords using the knowledge we already have. *If this, therefore this.* Rather than adding a fourth note to a triad to make a 7th chord, instead we can lower the root note to the 7th.

Let that sink in for a minute.

Say we want to play a major 7 chord. We can take *any* of the major triad shapes we know and lower the root note a semitone. This gives us a 7 3 5 voicing, which makes the sound of a major 7 chord.

The first exercise uses the G major triads you're now very familiar with and turns them into major 7 chords with lowered root voicings. Because you know these shapes, we won't beat about the bush here, we'll tackle all three of the main positions in one go!

These voicings aren't hugely useful on the lower strings, but on the higher strings they're magic.

Example 5a:

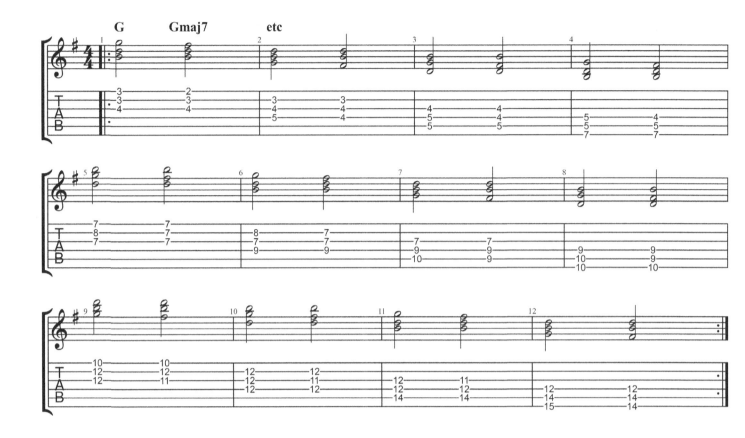

If we lower the root note of a major triad a tone, then we have a b7 3 5 voicing – a dominant 7.

Not only is an exercise like this great for developing chord vocabulary, it's incredible for drilling interval awareness. You'll never struggle to find the 7 and b7 again after this.

NB: a couple of these voicings turn out to be a little awkward to finger but that's OK. We don't have to use them all in practice, we're just exploring the neck.

Example 5b:

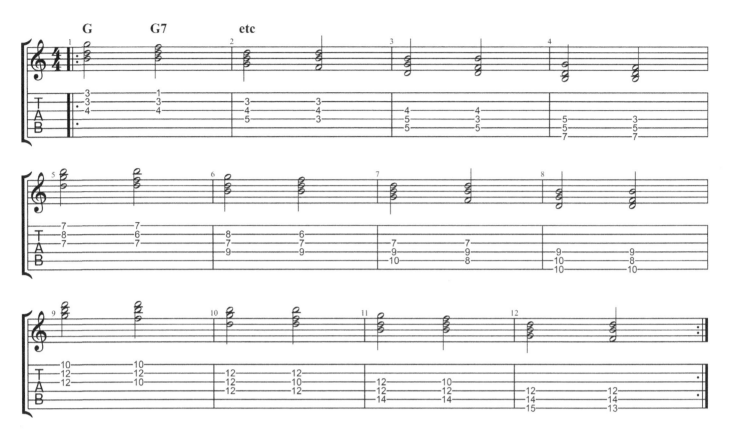

As you might have guessed, we can do the same exercise with a minor triad as our starting point. If we lower the root note of a minor triad by a tone, we have a b7 b3 5 voicing – a minor 7 chord.

This exercise uses the G minor triad shapes you're familiar with and lowers the root notes to play Gm7 voicings.

Example 5c:

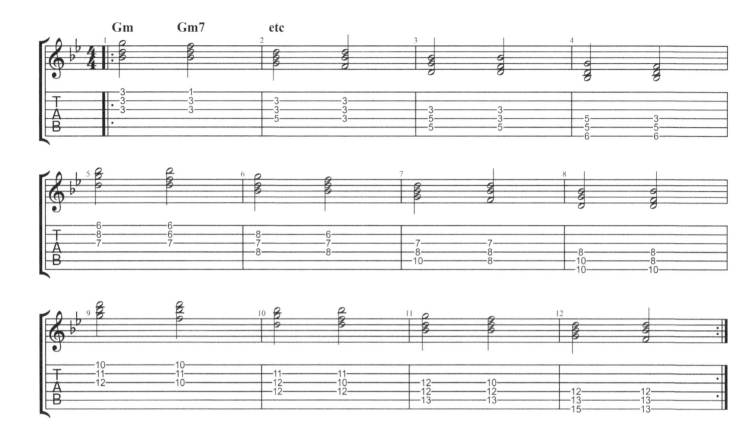

There is one chord in the harmonised major scale we've not covered yet – the minor 7b5. While this chord type doesn't come up too often (unless you're playing a lot of jazz), it's still worth looking at.

The minor 7b5 is built from the 7th degree of the major scale and based on a diminished triad. We worked on these in Routine Two (see Example 2d), where we noted that we can use a minor triad to form a diminished triad by flattening the 5th.

So, if it makes sense to you, think about a minor triad, flatten its 5th, then lower its root by a tone, and you'll have a b7 b5 b3 voicing – a minor 7b5.

However, that's a lot of steps to think through, so it's far better if you just know your diminished triads well enough that you can simply lower the root notes.

This exercise moves between Gdim and Gm7b5 voicings.

Example 5d:

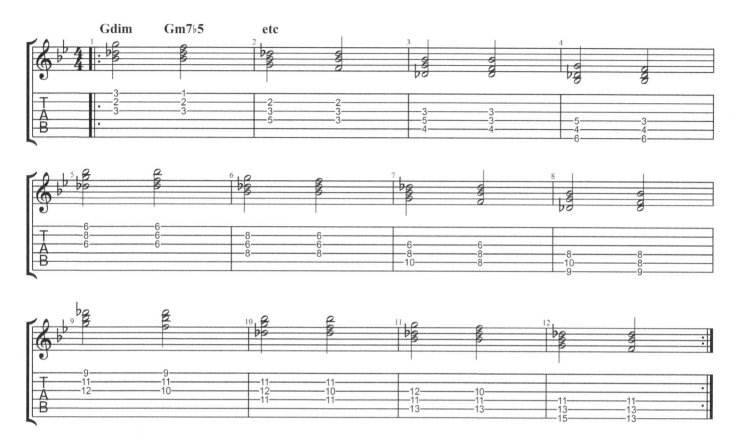

Before we move on, let's apply the new voicings we've looked at to some chord progressions and see how much we can achieve using triad visualisation skills.

First, a progression I included in the previous book in this series because it reminds me of sunny summer days. This time, the guitar playing is more pianistic.

There are lots of ways to practice this skill. You could play through the whole progression using regular triads, then go through it again playing lowered root voicings. Or you could play a triad then a lowered root voicing for each chord as you go. Alternatively, if you're feeling confident, you could just jump in and play the whole thing using only lowered root voicings. The more you practice, the easier it will become.

Example 5e:

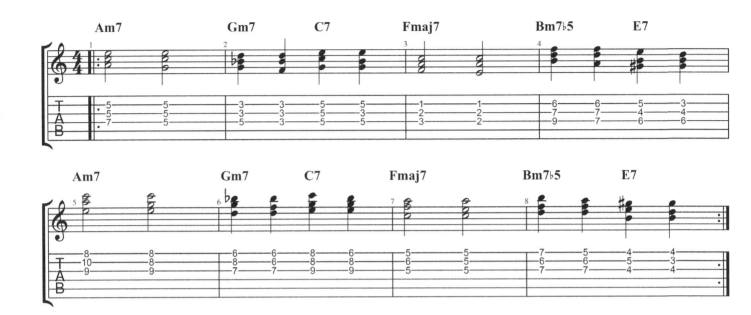

Here's a darker, more misty chord progression (also featured in the previous book) played using the same approach.

Example 5f:

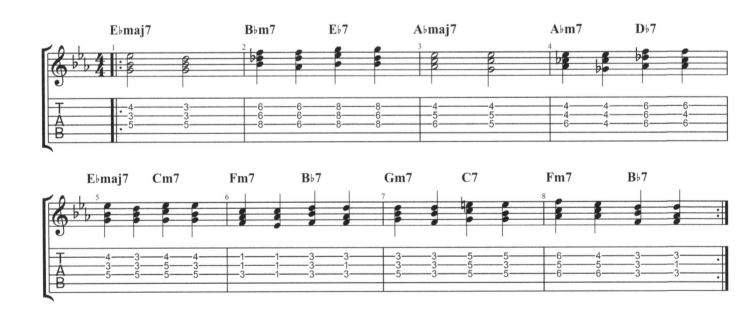

Next, I want to show you the *other way* I like to make my 7th chord voicings!

We've tackled lowered root voicings, now we'll move onto my favourites, *raised 5th* voicings.

As the name implies, this involves raising the 5th in a triad to move it up to the 7th, giving us a 1 3 7 voicing – a guide tone voicing. Voiced this way, these shapes sound OK, but when we invert them to play 3 7 1 or 7 1 3, we get a beautiful dissonance between the 7th and the root of the chord that makes it sound like we *really* know what we're doing!

This exercise moves between G major triads and raised 5th G major 7 voicings. The 7th is located four frets above the 5th, and this makes for some very wide stretches. Often that means repositioning your hand and re-fingering the chord. However, some of these are just not practical to play in the real world, so don't kill yourself!

Example 5g:

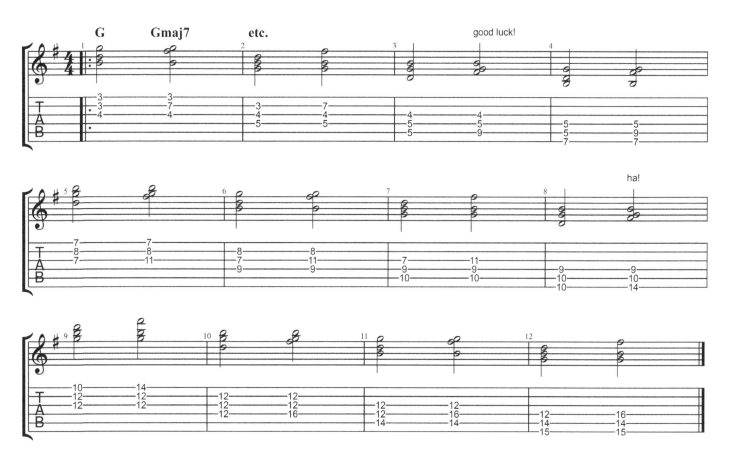

Let's apply the same idea to G major triads to create raised 5th G7 voicings. Again, this sometimes results in big stretches that you may not be able to reach, but as long as you can *see* the voicing, then you're improving your fretboard skills.

Example 5h:

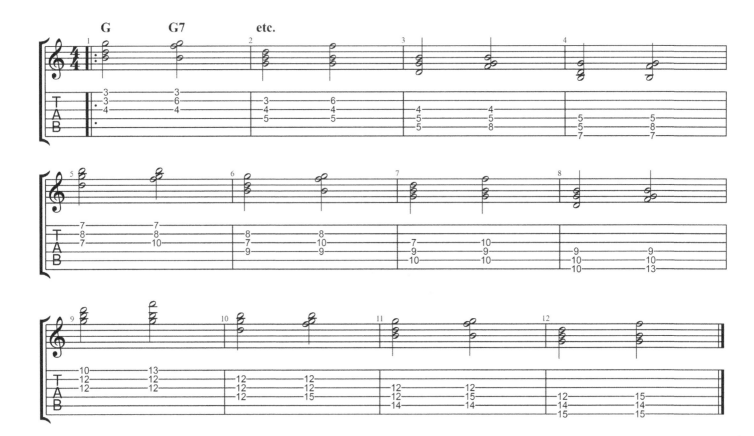

Now it's time to do the same with the minor 7 triad, but I have great news! Because this process means we end up with chords that don't contain the 5th, these voicings are perfectly fine to be used as m7b5 chords too! Half the work, double the use!

Example 5i:

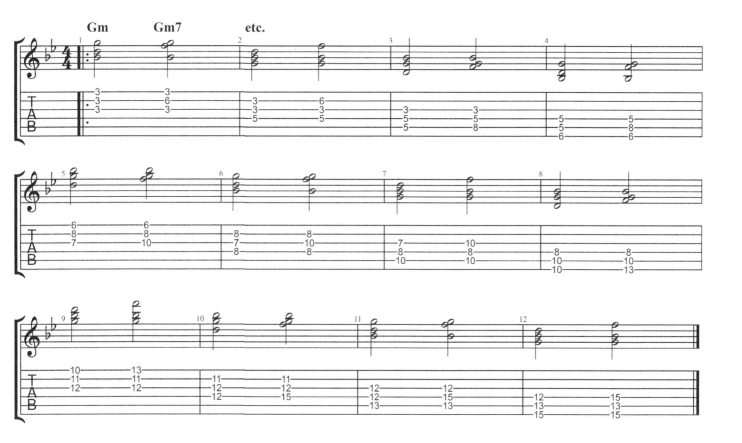

Let's put these voicings to work using the same two progressions as before. We can swap out some of the lowered root voicings for raised 5th ones. There are no rules here other than what appeals to our ears. I opted for voicings that fell under my fingers and kept my movement around the neck to a minimum.

Part of your practice routine should include coming up with different routes through the progression each time you play it. There's only so much you can learn from copying what I tell you to play – 50% of the value is found in just exploring the neck for yourself.

Example 5j:

And here's the same approach taken with our ballad progression.

Example 5k:

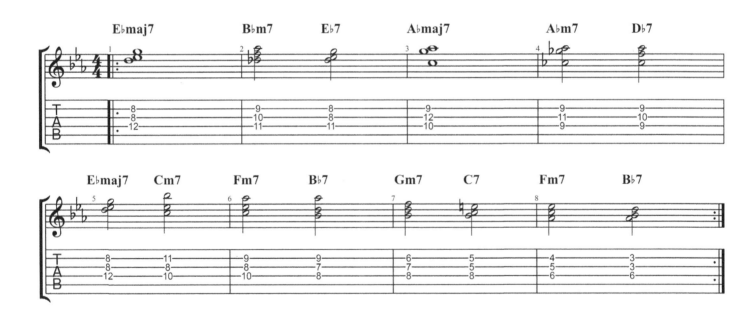

Before we end this routine, let me remind you that chords serve melodies. Although we've been working on chords, what we've *really* been working on is learning where different intervals live around triad voicings.

With this knowledge we can play all sorts of chords, but we can also add these notes into our melodies and pentatonic playing to bring more colour to our lines.

For example, the following line played over a G7 uses the b7 a lot. Now you should be able to spot it *and* hear it.

Example 5l:

Remember, there's no rush with this stuff. This is a practice routine not a lesson and I'm showing you things I practice with my more advanced students. They know this stuff already, but routines like these keep them in shape. If this is all new to you, it may take several weeks to master, but there are no shortcuts to making you the player you want to be… well, none worth taking!

See you on the next routine!

Routine Six – Major & Minor Pentatonic Drills

So far, we have focused on triads, 7th chords and seven-note scales – all useful tools to have in our arsenal, but there is always more. No musician is complete without access to their trusty pentatonic scales.

Despite often being one of the first things guitar players learn, pentatonic scales are almost never mastered. It's nice to be able to fall back on minor pentatonic shape one, but can you solo over major chords using different major pentatonic shapes? Or use pentatonic scales as substitutions over different chords to create more harmonically interesting sounds? Or access some of the five-note scale alternatives to the common minor and major pentatonic?

Well, we're going to help you get all of that fixed this week.

Let's start with the common minor pentatonic. It has the formula,

1 b3 4 5 b7

First of all, what do you see when you consider those intervals?

What smaller structures can you identify in there?

You'll immediately spot the minor triad (1 b3 5) but there is a really easy way of looking at this scale. It's a minor 7 arpeggio (1 b3 5 b7) with the addition of a 4th.

Let's warm up by playing the G Minor Pentatonic scale in the CAGED E shape. You probably know this shape very well, so focus on the intervals while playing it. Some intervals (like the 1 and b3) are much more pleasing to land on than others (the 4 or 5).

Example 6a:

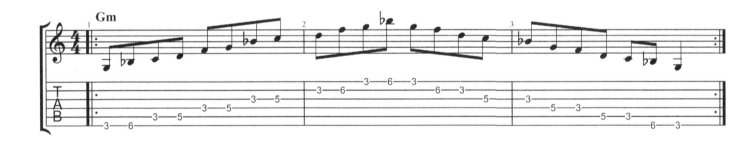

This is the most common box pattern for the minor pentatonic that everyone learns, but there are four other patterns. If you're unfamiliar with the other shapes, we have to fix that next.

The next exercise runs up and down each of the patterns in G minor. You goal is to visualise and learn each one in relation to a root note on the low E or A string (and, in the case of one pattern, on the D string. Yuk!)

You've already played the E shape with its root on the low E string, played with the first finger.

The D shape is rooted on the D string, played with the first finger.

The C shape is rooted on the A string, but we use the third or fourth finger for the root note. I think of these as *backward shapes*. There's a root note, but the other notes are behind rather than in front of it.

The A shape is rooted on the A string with the first finger.

The G shape is rooted on the low E string and is another backward shape, so the root is played with the third or fourth finger.

Example 6b:

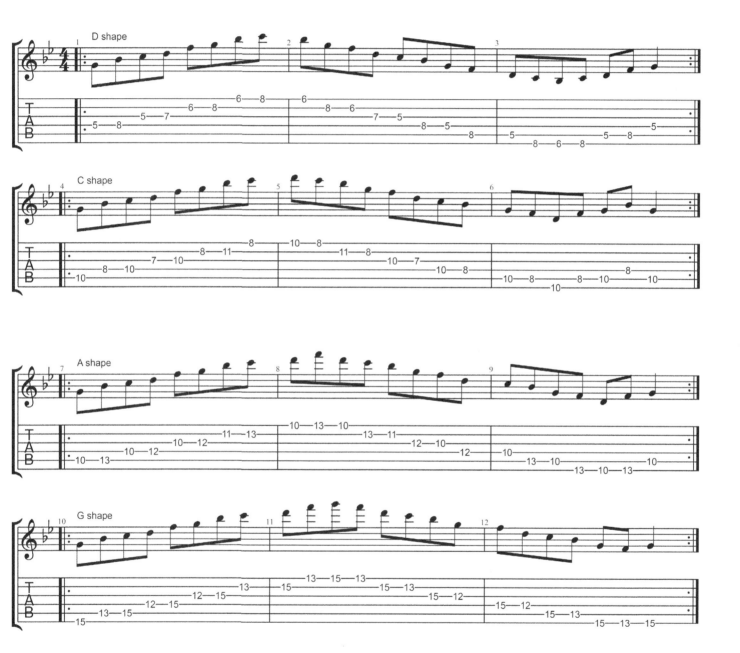

An exercise like this is good for checking you definitely know the shapes, but I don't like it! We're just playing them in order, and it feels like we know each shape with less confidence than the previous one.

Instead, we need a way of practicing the scale without any kind of bias. We're going to do that right now by using the following chord progression:

Gm7 – Bbm7 – Cm7 – Ebm7 – Fm7

That might appear to be an arbitrary, quite un-musical progression, but when we apply it to the fretboard, we can play all five of those pentatonic scales without really having to move our fretting hand. This allows us to focus purely on finding a root note and superimposing the relevant scale shape over it.

We start in the E shape for G Minor Pentatonic and ascend/descend the scale. In order to move to Bb Minor Pentatonic, we visualise the root note on the low E string, 6th fret. In order to remain in position, we use the G shape, which has its root note on the low E, and is a "backward" shape, with the notes arranged below the root, and play this shape starting with the fourth finger at the 6th fret.

As we play up and down that scale, next we're looking for C Minor Pentatonic. We find the root note on the A string, 3rd fret, and play it in the A shape. Then it's Eb Minor Pentatonic, played from the root note on the A string, 6th fret, so that's the C shape. Finally, F Minor Pentatonic is launched from the D string, 3rd fret in the D shape.

Play through it now!

Example 6c:

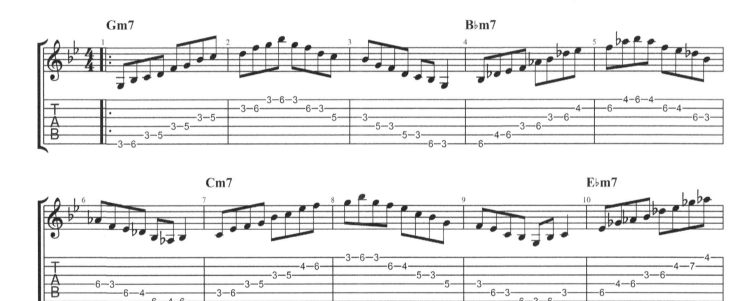

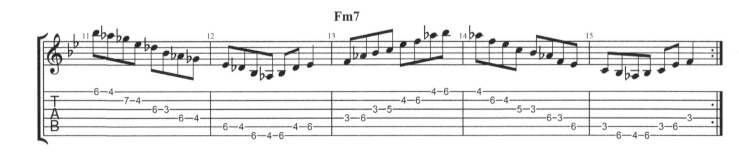

Now we can mix that up and start off in the C shape of G Minor Pentatonic and play all five scales again! The skill we are training here is to be able to look ahead and see where we need to go while we're still playing over the previous chord. I think of this as developing RAM speed – the ability to forget what we're doing and focus on what we're going to be doing next.

Example 6d:

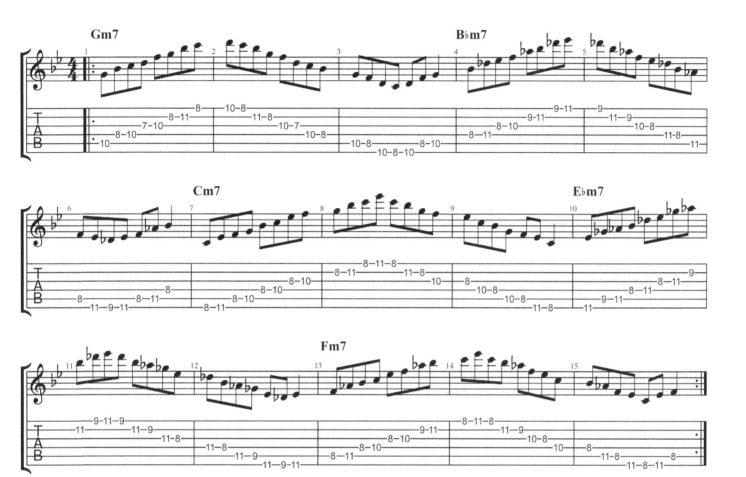

Let's do that again, this time starting in the A shape of G Minor Pentatonic.

Example 6e:

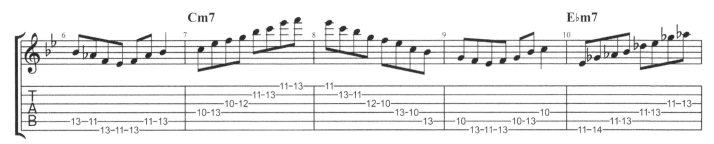

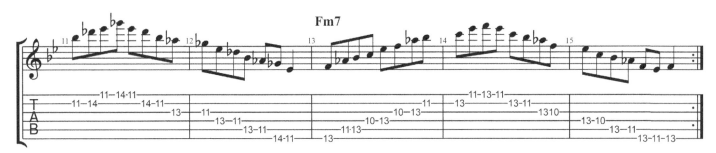

There are, of course, two more pathways through this but I won't bore you with them. We don't have enough space to include them, plus you can't say you know this stuff unless you can work it out for yourself, without me holding your hand. I believe in you!

What I do want to briefly look at, however, is the same approach using G Major Pentatonic. Some are reading this and thinking, "But, Levi, if I need to play major, I'll just play the minor pentatonic three frets lower!" While it's true we can do that, it's a shortcut – and shortcuts are rarely without their shortcomings.

If you have good minor pentatonic vocabulary, when you play it three frets lower it'll just sound like minor vocabulary played in the wrong place, and I know you don't want that! We're advancing guitarists here, we should be able to handle major sounds too.

The major pentatonic formula is 1 2 3 5 6. It's a major triad with an added 2nd and 6th. It sounds simple because it is. If you know your major triads well, you can do this!

First, let's play G Major Pentatonic in the E shape.

Example 6f:

Now, here are the other four major pentatonic scale shapes in one exercise. Don't rush through these – it's important to know these shapes really well and be able to automatically play each one from the root. The fingerings will be exactly the same as they were for the minor pentatonic shapes.

Example 6g:

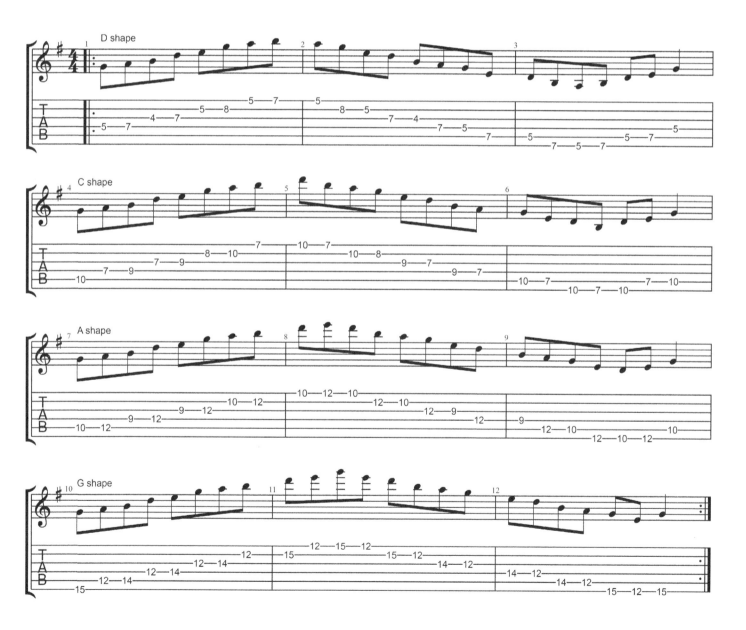

Now that we've played both minor and major pentatonic shapes in the same positions on the fretboard, it's easier to compare G major to G minor. Now, *that* is worth our time. That's parallel modal thinking, when we compare scales to the same root note so we can see how they differ.

For example, how are G Major Pentatonic (G A B D E) and E Minor Pentatonic (E G A B D) different? Well, they're not really…

But compare G Major Pentatonic (G A B D E) with G Minor Pentatonic (G Bb C D F) and now you can really see the difference.

As was the case with the minor, I want you to *really know* the major patterns and how to find them, so we'll turn to the major chord version of the progression we used earlier, so that we can run through five major pentatonic scales in one zone of the neck:

Gmaj – Bbmaj – Cmaj – Ebmaj – Fmaj

We're starting in the E shape of G Major Pentatonic.

Example 6h:

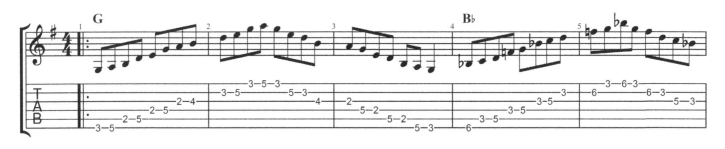

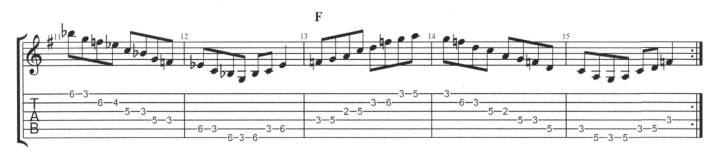

Here's the same idea starting in the C shape. On the audio you'll hear me saying the name of the chord/scale I'm going to before I get there. I'm using my visualisation skills to find it before I need to play it, so that there aren't any gaps in my playing.

This stuff takes time, but when you get it? Well, it feels like a super power!

Example 6i:

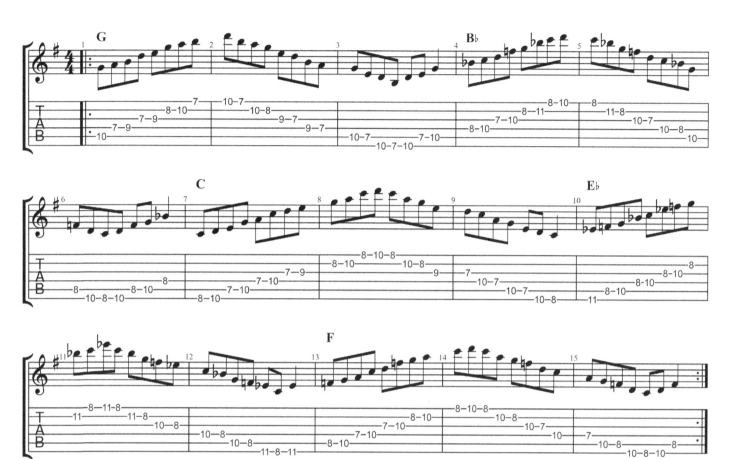

Here's the same idea, but now starting in the A shape. We're keeping you on your toes, always looking for the next position. This is a real brain workout!

Example 6j:

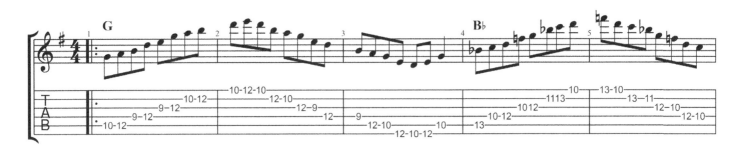

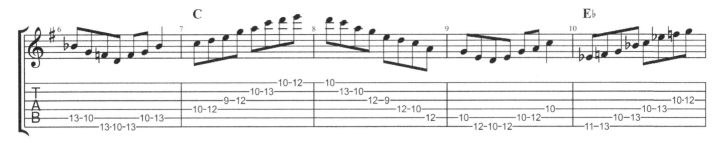

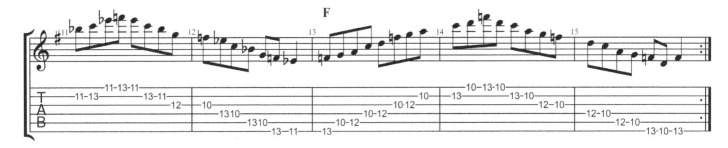

To end this routine, I want to remind you that the pentatonic scales we've played so far have been the most common sounds, but they're not the only pentatonic scales out there. The question is, should we learn more scales as brute force memory tests, or can we use what we already know to help us learn other things?

There is a minor pentatonic variation that some people call the minor 6 pentatonic. I've also heard it called the Robben Ford pentatonic.

What is it?

It's like the minor pentatonic scale, but instead of a b7 it has a 6th, which gives the scale a really nice, jazzy or funky sound.

So, it's a new scale, sure, but what if we approach it from the perspective of what we already know? *If this, therefore this*.

Thought of in this way, the 6th will always be a semitone below the b7.

This example takes the minor pentatonic shape you already know and turns it into G Minor 6 Pentatonic by replacing the b7 with the 6th.

Not only does this approach take the workload off the brain, it really makes it clear which note gives this scale it's flavour because it's based around a very familiar shape. Now, you can focus on it more easily when soloing.

Example 6k:

I could go through every position of this, but that's not the point (and we'd soon run out of space!) The point is being able to *find* these sounds for yourself, so let's look at another pentatonic scale.

Steve Khan has written about the "dominant pentatonic" scale. He built it as a major pentatonic scale, but with a b7 replacing the 6th.

Here's G Dominant Pentatonic.

Example 6l:

Finally, here's one I've also seen called dominant pentatonic, although Shaun Baxter once referred to it as the Rogan Pentatonic. It's a minor pentatonic scale, but with the b3 replaced with a major 3rd to create a more pleasing major sound.

This one is fun as it has wide, pentatonic-like intervals, like the minor 3rd distance between the 5th and b7, as well as crunchier sounds like the semitone between the 3rd and 4th.

Example 6m:

We're barely scratching the surface of the pentatonic options available to us. There could easily be a whole book's worth of content that explores the technique and application of other interesting pentatonic sounds. However, there's enough here to keep you busy for at least a week.

Get to work and I'll see you next time!

Routine Seven – Triads & 7ths, In Position… and Out!

Now we're getting into the heavy lifting section of the book – the part where we really abandon the easier things we might have relied upon and open up the fretboard in ways we've only dreamt of.

What do I mean by that, exactly?

I'm sure you know the feeling of being led by your limitations on the instrument, right?

To give a simple example, let's say you only know one voicing of B7. Anytime you need to play a B7, no matter where you are on the neck, you have to jump back into that one shape you know! You might do the same thing with scales. No matter where you're playing rhythm on the neck, when it's time for you to solo, you're forced to jump up to the E shape of the minor pentatonic scale, because that's all you know.

You get the picture…

With a bit more thought, a bit more exploration, and a bit more (dare I say it) *practice*, no matter where you are on the neck you *can* play the sound you need.

Back in Routine Two, we looked at how to play the triads of the major scale in one area of the neck, rather than shifting up for each chord. Let's quickly review that.

Here's a G Major chord scale played as triads, keeping our hands positioned around the 3rd fret area.

Example 7a:

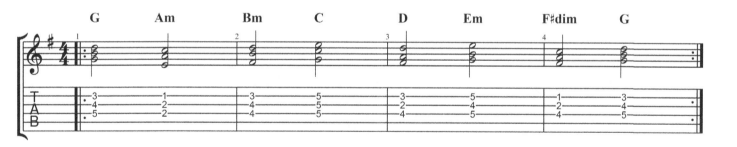

In this week's routine, we're going to focus more on melodic content than chords, but everything will still be based on our triad knowledge as the foundation.

In this first exercise, we're playing little triad arpeggios to open up the fretboard.

First, we can take one shape and move it up the neck to spell out every chord in the harmonised scale.

Example 7b:

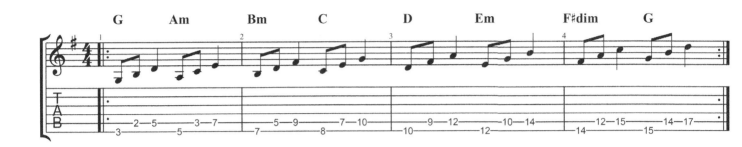

But we can also play triad arpeggios while remaining in one area of the neck.

There are many different ways to develop this skill, but now seems like a good time to remind you: we're thinking intervals here, not pitches.

I know that the second chord in the chord-scale is A minor, but I never think, "OK, A minor contains the notes A, C and E" because I don't need to.

Instead, I play the root note, then I think b3 interval (because the chord is minor). In Example 7c I played the low E string root note of Am with my fourth finger, so I know the b3 must be on the A string.

From there, where is the 5th? I could move up on the A string, but I want to stay in the same region of the neck, so I reach for it on the D string.

Chord iii is B minor. We know where the root is, so where are the b3 and 5th?

Then C major. Where's the root, the 3rd, the 5th? Etc…

In the early stages of your development, this will feel like pulling teeth, but we're training ourselves to think in a different way. In time, this will be effortless.

Example 7c:

We've played these arpeggios in an ascending fashion but we can mix that up. Using the same chord scale, let's alternate between ascending and descending the triads.

This requires more thought than playing a repeating ascending pattern and I find it helps to literally say out loud, "Up G major, down A minor, up B minor…" etc. The goal here is to really know the triads you're playing, not just run through a fingering pattern.

Example 7d:

Let's move into a different zone of the neck and play ascending triads using the G shape. Saying the name of each triad before you play it will help you focus on the task.

Example 7e:

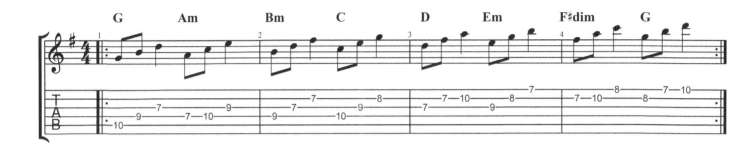

Thus far, we've been working these ideas very much "within the grid". In other words, our triads have been played over two beats, so that each new triad starts on a new beat.

To break this up, I want us to work on a "three against four" rhythmic device to make the triads sound a little more interesting.

The following example moves from playing four notes on the low E and A string, to playing three notes on both strings. So, we have two bars of a predictable pattern, followed by two bars where the note groups don't line up with the beat to create rhythmic interest.

Example 7f:

If we then take this pattern and apply it to our ascending triads, we get a far more interesting sound – one that ends up sounding much more musical, despite its formulaic nature.

Example 7g:

We can also mix directions and even positions when doing this, as shown in the next example.

Example 7h:

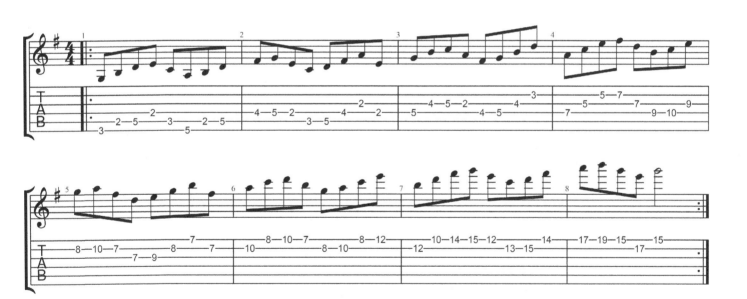

It makes sense that we should explore this idea using 7th chords as well as triads. First, let's just try ascending the arpeggios in one position. As with the previous examples, I want you to really engage your brain here. Say to yourself, "G major 7, A minor 7, B minor 7, C major 7" and so on.

If at this point you're thinking, "That doesn't help me", just pause and consider that fact. Knowing basic 7th chords and being able to locate them on the neck should be simple, and if it's not then you've got some homework to do. I'm presenting them here because I *want* that frustration in your/my practice. It's the only way to advance. We should be able to do this, and this fact can drive us to work on it.

Example 7i:

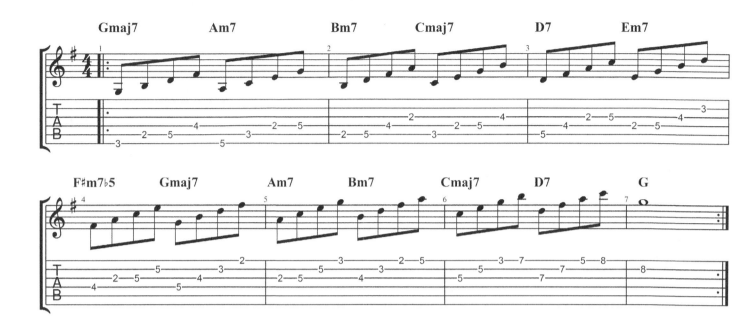

Here's another example, this time using the A shape. We could spend time drilling this all over the neck, but again, you know this! If we wrote out every possibility, this book would be 400 pages long!

Example 7j:

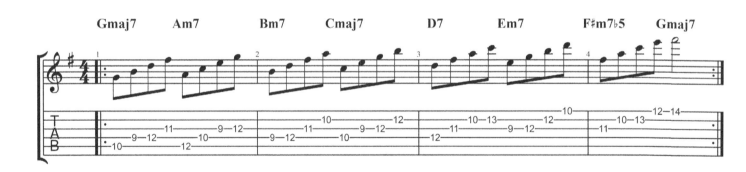

Let's start to break positions. Real mastery of the fretboard comes via flexibility rather than rigidity. We should be free to move around the fretboard at will, breaking out of boxes when necessary.

Here we're playing two different ascending G major 7 arpeggios. These are just two of the many possible ways to play an extended arpeggio.

Example 7k:

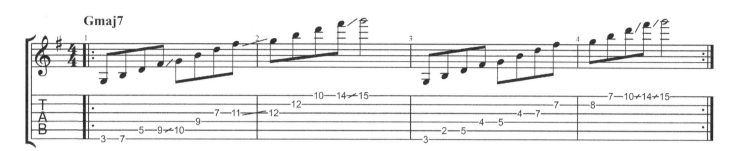

Finally, I want us to play through our G major chord scale, covering three full octaves for each chord. This requires some positional knowledge as we transition from one area of the neck to the next. I'm not thinking of the notes of the arpeggios at all, but I am thinking, "OK, now I need to shift up to the C shape" and "here's a good place to transition into the next area" etc.

Example 7l:

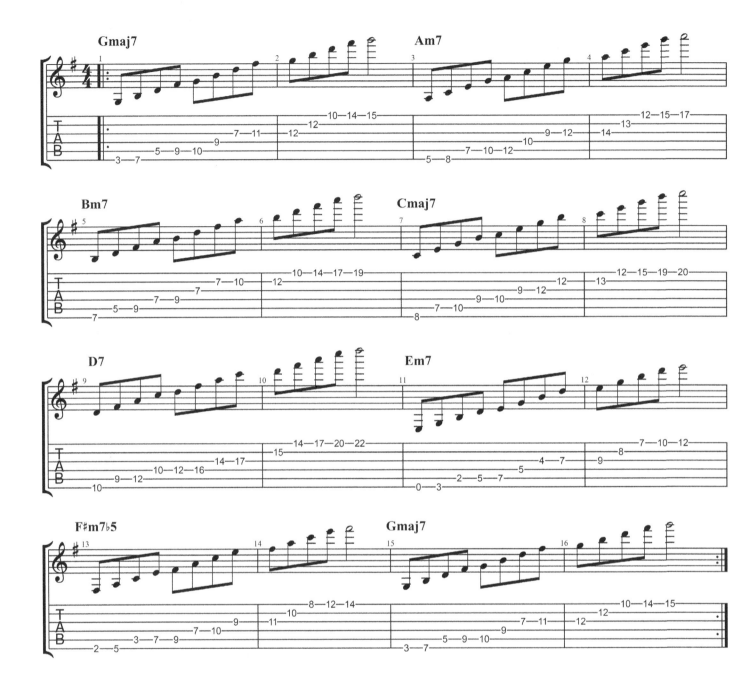

There's a lot to work in here, so get to it and I'll see you in a week!

Routine Eight – Open Voiced Triads & Chord Melody

If you're thinking we've done all there is to do with triads/chords, well we're genuinely only scratching the surface of music harmony, let alone engaging in the struggle to apply this knowledge on our instrument!

In this chapter we're going to take another step forward by focusing on *open voiced triads*. These are a twist on the triads we've already practiced and present all manner of technical challenges while creating some wonderful new sounds we can use in our playing.

What's an open voiced triad?

So far, when playing triads, we've always played the notes in order. If we were playing a G major triad, we'd play G, B then D, and those notes would fit within one octave.

An open voiced triad throws that out of the window. Instead, we can play the G, skip over the B, play the D, then add the B on top. Rather than the notes being arranged on adjacent strings, now we're skipping a string to add the final note. This creates a more open, spacious sound than the closed voice triad.

So, here we're going to play some open voiced triads that are created by taking the middle note of a closed voice triad and moving it up or down an octave.

As an example, here's a closed voiced G major triad that we'll turn into an open voiced one. First, we take the middle note (B) and relocate it down an octave, then up an octave. They both sound great right?

Example 8a:

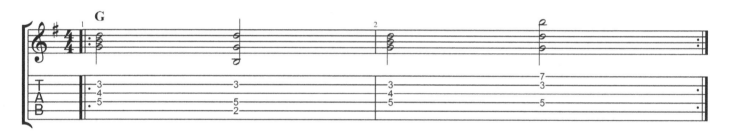

I've found that the best way to learn these shapes is to play them up and down in position. In the E shape, there are four shapes we can cycle through.

In this example I'm strumming the chords where possible, but where there is more than one string being skipped, this becomes tricky without very good fretting hand muting. For these shapes, hybrid picking (combining pick and fingers) is easier. (If you're new to this technique, I cover it in depth in my hybrid picking book!)

Example 8b:

When doing the same exercise in the C shape we run into the same problem when strumming. I'm using my pick and fingers here.

Example 8c:

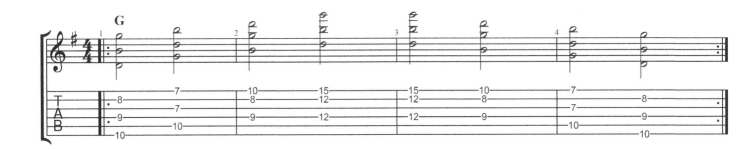

Finally, here are open voiced G major triads in the A shape.

Example 8d:

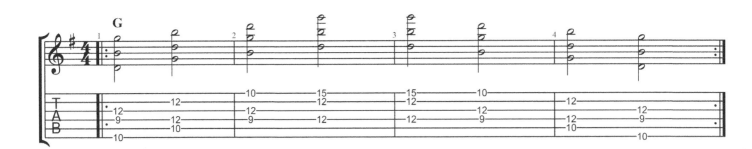

All of these triads can be arpeggiated and played with alternate picking too. Let's jump back down to the E shape and try that, but this time playing G minor instead of G major triads.

There's a lot of skill required in this level of alternate picking as we need to jump between picking adjacent and skipped strings. Take this slowly at first and build up the speed over time.

Example 8e:

We can also play open voiced triads along the strings rather than in position. Here are G minor triads arranged on the A, D and B strings, ascending the neck, then continuing on the D, G and high E strings.

Example 8f:

Open voiced triads have formed part of the playing style of numerous great players over the years, most appear most notably in the chordal work of the incredible Eric Johnson, and the ferocious classical inspired picking of Steve Morse.

Here is a Morse-style alternate picking pattern that moves through a chord progression. When Steve plays things like this, it's usually four times faster than we're doing it here! But we're not looking for speed yet, just understanding and control. Few people will ever have the technical proficiency to play things like this at Steve's speeds, but we can absolutely take and use the concepts in our own playing.

Example 8g:

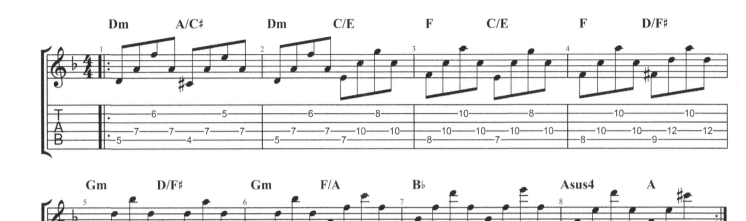

One of the most ear opening aspects of these open sounding triads is how we can turn our chord work into ideas that incorporate both melody and range.

There's an undeniable jazz/gospel edge to these ideas (something useful to me in my soul band) but I think these sorts of things have a lot in common with a more tender, ballad style of piano playing.

In this example we're playing a Gm7 chord then using just the pinkie finger to play an ascending melody while still holding down the chord. Make sure the notes ring out as much as possible.

Example 8h:

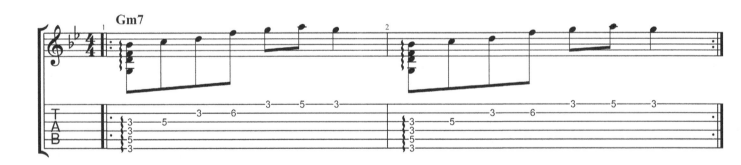

We can do something similar around the A shape too, but this time the middle and pinkie fingers are required to move. It requires a fair amount of control to keep some fingers static while moving others to play a melody, but you will develop that level of control over time.

Example 8i:

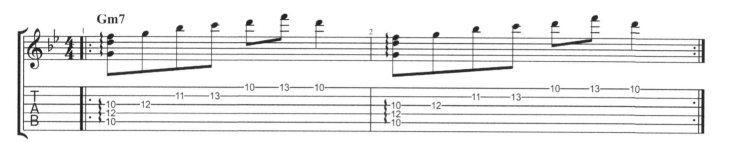

The next example uses the A shape for a major 7 voicing and adds a melody on the B and high E strings, then shifts to another inversion of the major 7 chord and completes the melody.

Example 8j:

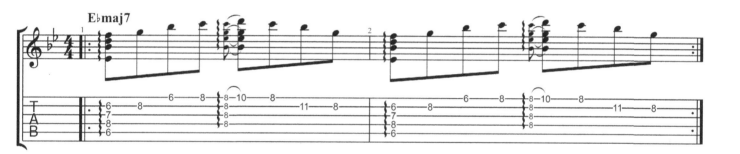

This example uses three different G major voicings, starting in the E shape, moving into the C shape, and ending up in the A shape. Again, the notes accessible around the chord forms are used to create the melody.

Example 8k:

Here's a similar idea but now based around a Cm7 chord. We start down in the A shape, transition into the E shape, then use one of our open voiced triads as a way of transitioning into the A shape we began with, an octave higher.

Example 81:

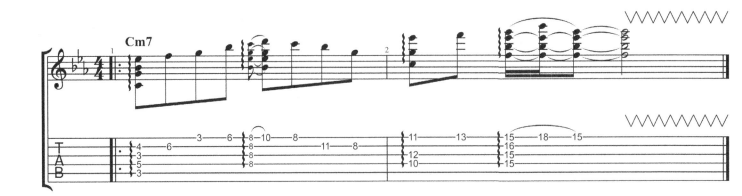

The ideas here are just scratching the surface of what's possible. Use them as a springboard for your own studies to advance your rhythm and melody playing.

Whether you want to get into the otherworldly rock playing of someone like Andy Timmons, or the Neo-Soul vibes of players like Jairus Mozee or Jubu Smith, how you connect and embellish your chords will play a big part in shaping your sound.

If thoroughly explored, the ideas here will help push you far beyond the old 12-bars blues patterns you're probably bored to death of!

Get practicing and I'll see you next week!

Routine Nine – Modal Control

This week it's time to focus on modes and what they mean for our visualisation of chords/scales, plus the best way for us to practice them.

Thanks to guitar magazines and the internet, modes are a favourite subject amongst guitarists. Almost every young student tells their guitar teacher they want to learn about the modes – way before they need to know anything about them – and because of this, a subject that should be approached later, when it would be easy, becomes more like Pythagoras than music!

So far in this series of books we've covered the Ionian (major scale), Mixolydian and Dorian modes, but let's remind ourselves what a mode actually is.

If you look at a die that you might use to play a board game, it has six sides. You could say that it has six *modes* in which it can appear when rolled. This is like the major scale.

We have the major scale that we're all very familiar with, but there are six other aspects to it. Depending on which note we place on the bottom the scale will sound different.

A G Major scale sounds like G Major when played over a G bass note. Change that note to an A, however, and suddenly everything sounds different. The C note that sounded like a 4th interval over G, now sounds minor, because it's the b3 of A minor. It's all about the intervals.

Because this is an advanced book, we're not going to relate the modes back to a parent scale – that's no help to anyone. Instead, we'll compare each mode to the benchmark of the major scale and look at how the intervals differ, and we'll play each scale from the same G root note.

There are two key bits of knowledge you should leave this chapter with:

1. Which modes relate to which chords in a scale.

2. An understanding of the "character" notes that really bring out the sound of each mode.

Let's get to work!

First, let's play the G Ionian mode, more commonly known as the major scale. This is the bedrock against which we compare every other scale.

It has the formula: 1 2 3 4 5 6 7

Example 9a:

Although scales are usually taught in a linear fashion, I encourage my students to think vertically, because it can really help us to get what a mode *sounds* like if we can visualise/hear it as a chord.

The Ionian is like a major 7 chord (1 3 5 7) with an added 9th, 11th and 13th. The 11th is quite dissonant, and we can only practically play a maximum of six notes on guitar, so we could say that it sounds like a major 13 chord.

If we stack up the intervals 1 3 5 7 9 11 13, this is what we get:

Example 9b:

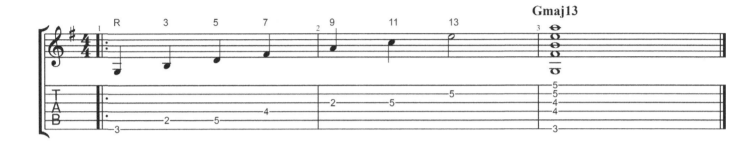

This is a great skill to practice, so that you can do it anywhere on the neck. Here's the same idea based around the A shape. Practice it in all positions.

Example 9c:

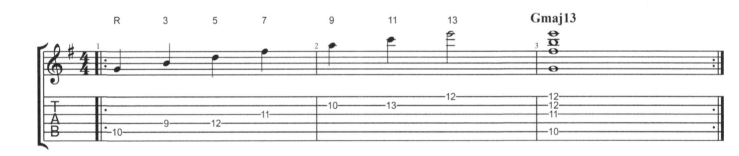

The second mode of the major scale is the Dorian mode.

The Dorian mode has the formula: 1 2 b3 4 5 6 b7

In other words, it's like a major scale but with a b3 and b7.

We can play this as a linear scale, but let's also get the sound of it in our ears by stacking it vertically, expressed as a chord.

Dorian is like a minor 7 chord (1 b3 5 b7) with an added 9th, 11th and 13th, so it makes the sound of a minor 13 chord.

The natural 6th of the Dorian (combined with its b3) is really important, because that's its character note, which helps us to differentiate it from other minor modes.

Example 9d:

Let's combine the G Ionian and G Dorian modes to play a modal musical example. Notice that I'm making a point of playing notes that really highlight the quality of the mode we're playing.

Example 9e:

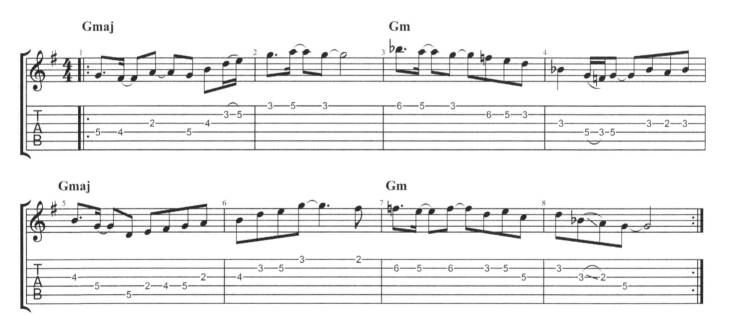

The third mode of the major scale is the Phrygian mode.

It has the formula: 1 b2 b3 4 5 b6 b7

It's like a major scale with a b2, b3, b6 and b7.

The b2 (a.k.a. b9) is the important character note of this scale.

To represent the sound of this scale in a chord, we stack up the intervals 1 b3 5 b7 b9 11 b13 which make the sound of a 7sus4b9 chord.

Phrygian isn't a hugely common mode compared to some of the others, but any time you want to play over a minor chord built on the third degree of the scale, Phrygian has the note choices you want.

Let's play it first as a scale, then vertically, spelling out G7sus4b9.

Example 9f:

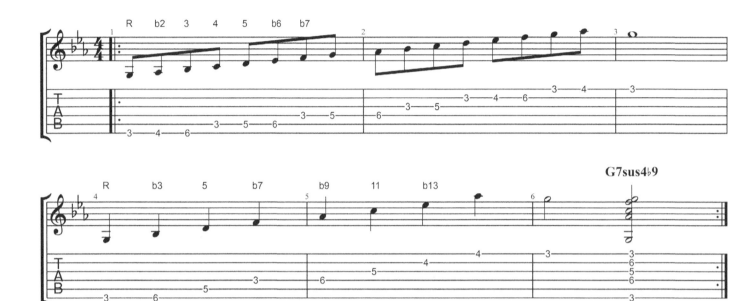

The fourth mode of the major scale is the Lydian mode. It has the formula:

1 2 3 #4 5 6 7

It's nice and easy compared to the Phrygian!

Lydian is like a major scale with a raised 4th. In other words, it's a major 7 chord (1 3 5 7) with an added 9th, #11 and 13th. That's a major 13#11 or just a major7#11 chord – a wonderfully dreamy sound.

Lydian's character notes are the 3rd and 7th to give us the major 7 sound, plus its unique #11 colour tone.

Example 9g:

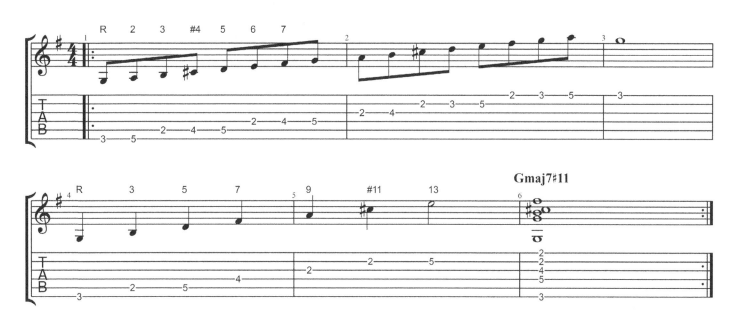

The fifth mode is another that we've already covered in this series. The Mixolydian mode has the formula:

1 2 3 4 5 6 b7

It's another nice, easy one – like a major scale with a b7.

Mixolydian is like a dominant 7 chord (1 3 5 b7) with an added 9th, 11th and 13th – a dominant 13 chord.

Its character notes are its 3rd and b7, which tell us it's a dominant scale. The other notes are nice, but it's the dominant function that is its most important aspect.

Example 9h:

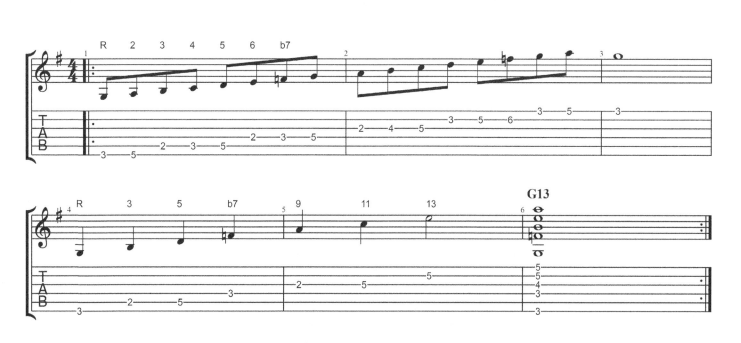

The sixth mode is the Aeolian, also known as the natural minor scale. It has the formula:

1 2 b3 4 5 b6 b7

Like the major scale, the Aeolian will be the basis of a lot of the music you play. Seen vertically as a chord, we can stack up the 1 b3 5 b7 9 11 b13 intervals.

This gives us a minor 7 chord (1 b3 5 b7) with an added 9th and 11th.

I've left out the b6 interval as it's really dark sounding and not something we'd include in a chord unless we were playing really contemporary jazz.

The character notes of this scale are the b3 and b7, and the b6 tells us that it's not the Dorian mode.

Example 9i:

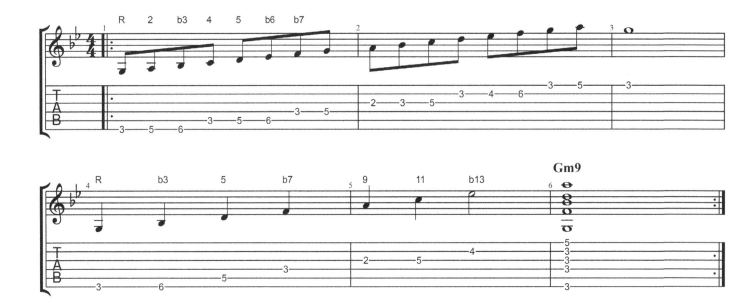

The final mode is the Locrian. This is a dark one! It has the formula:

1 b2 b3 4 b5 b6 b7

It's all of the darkest sounding intervals rolled into one, so it doesn't come up very often in mainstream music and is more the preserve of metal music and horror movie scores.

If we stack up the intervals 1 b3 b5 b7 b9 11 b13 we have a minor 7b5 chord (1 b3 b5 b7) plus the b9, 11th and b13 (a.k.a. the #5).

These additional notes are too dark, so we won't include them in the chord when practicing, we'll just use a minor 7b5.

The b2/b9 and b5 are the character notes of this scale, which help differentiate it from more common minor modes.

Example 9j:

Now let's mix some modes together! First, let's take a common chord progression that I've seen in numerous pop and rock tunes over the years. C – D – E – E

As popular as this progression is, all these chords don't belong to just one key. The C and D chords can be seen as belonging to the key of E Minor, in which they are chords VI and VII. Instead of following these with the expected Em7, however, we have an E major chord. This could be viewed as chord I in the key of E Major or chord V in the key of A Major. I hear it as the latter, so I play the Mixolydian mode over it.

In bars 1-2 of this example we'll play E Aeolian (natural minor) and move into E Mixolydian for bars 3-4, then repeat the process for the remaining four bars.

Example 9k:

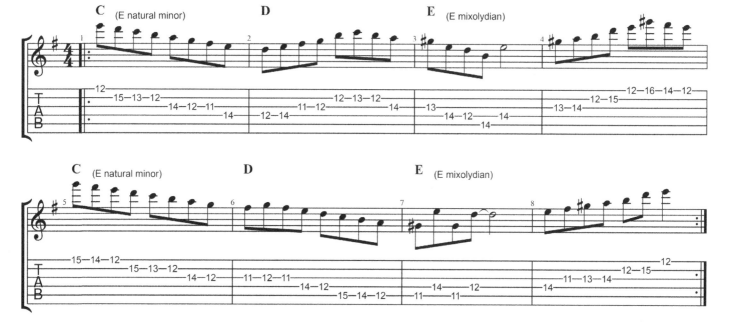

The previous example took a key centre approach to playing over changes, breaking the progression down into two tonal centres – E Minor and A Major – and playing the appropriate mode for each one.

We're going to end this routine with a long exercise that compares every mode over just one bass note. We're also changing key this time and playing the modes from a C root note.

This is a workout for our mind/ears as well as our fingers. It's the ideal way to compare modes and hear exactly how each one sounds.

For the book, I've written out the scales straight, ascending and descending. On the audio, you'll hear that after playing the scale, I improvise a little bit with each scale.

I chose not to TAB that out for you, because otherwise you'll just learn what I played and that would miss the point of the exercise. This is just a taster of the potential of each scale, and the important thing is that you go and explore them, and discover their sounds for yourself. You can jam on each mode for hours and see what ideas emerge. Make sure to focus on the character notes of each mode, referred to earlier – it's all about exploration!

Example 9l:

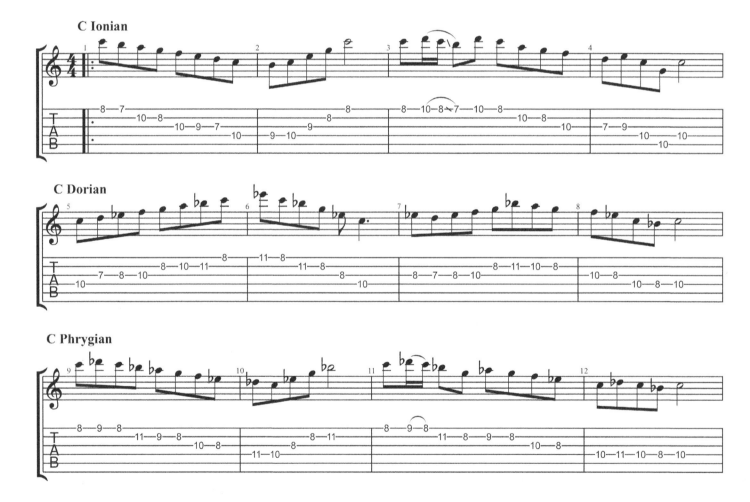

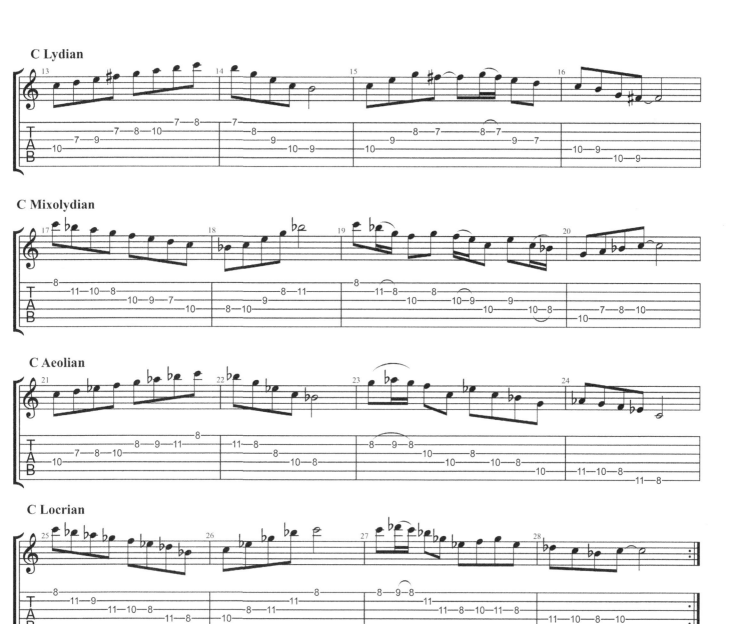

Once again, we've only scratched the surface here. We could devote months to expanding all these ideas, but if you've made it through this chapter without too much of struggle, then you've done well!

I'll see you in a week!

Routine Ten – Economy/Sweep Picking

We've spent nine weeks focusing primarily on fretboard knowledge and theory, but it's also been a covert study of alternate picking. Everything we've played has kept our picking hand pumping away, down up down up, ad infinitum.

I'm a firm believer that the alternate picking motion should be at the core of our playing. It's wonderful for rhythm and overall time feel. We can't possibly play out of time if we've developed the skill of keeping our picking hand moving up and down like a metronome. And if the music needs to swing, we just change our picking hand rhythm slightly to have a bit of swagger.

In almost 20 years of teaching guitar, I still see alternate picking as a weakness/flaw in students' technique. While we could keep on drilling the alternate picking motion, it's important to remember that technique is a broader subject with other aspects, so in this final routine we're going to delve into the world of sweep/ economy picking.

Economy picking involves using a sweeping motion to play a series of notes on adjacent strings. In certain musical situations, this gives us a far more "economical" way to play.

The first thing to note is that a sweep is one continuous motion – it's not a series of individual pick strokes. We're not really plucking the strings, we *push through* each string, so that our pick briefly rests on the next string (called a *rest stroke*).

Let me illustrate this first of all with a rake across a C major chord. In the following example you'll push through all six strings with a single downstroke.

We're not focused on timing here, just technique. Push your pick quickly through all six strings.

Example 10a:

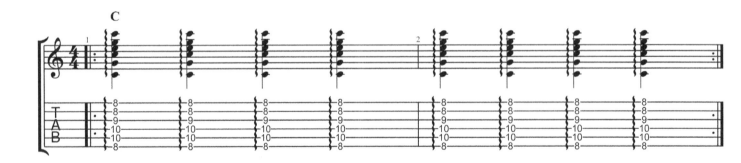

So, we've played the motion, pushing through the strings, now we just need to learn to control it. We'll start to do that by playing a simple ascending triplet across three strings.

We begin on the D string, ascend a C major triad, then ending with an upstroke on beat 2.

Focus on the downstroke beginning on beat 1 and the upstroke landing on beat 2. The rest should just even out.

Example 10b:

Now let's try a four-note grouping across the top four strings. Our goal is to get the rhythm as even as possible, so that each note is the same length, and the line is played smoothly. Rhythmic consistency is always the weak area of economy of motion because it's so easy to rush!

Example 10c:

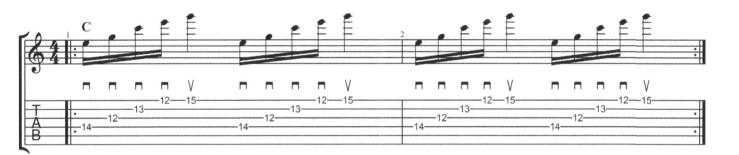

Sweep picking works in the opposite direction too, so we need to work on this motion with an upstroke. You'll find that you need to change the angle of your pick for this. When we sweep down, towards the ground, the pick is angled down, but when we change direction, we need to angle the pick up to pass smoothly over the strings.

Example 10d:

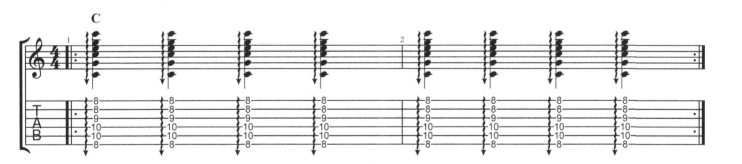

Let's use the triplet idea again, now starting with a descending motion. Once again, aim for a smooth, even rhythm.

Example 10e:

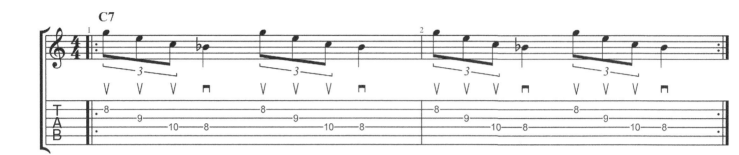

Once we're beginning to achieve an even rhythm on ascending and descending sweeps, we can start to practice changing direction mid-phrase. This exercise ascends a D minor triad then hits a high C to begin a descending sweep.

Example 10f:

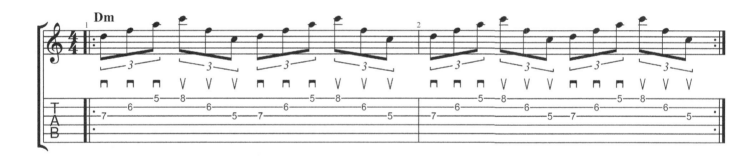

So far, our exercises have focused on direct string changes. Each change has been played with a sweeping motion, but in economy picking sometimes your string crossing will happen with an *inside* picking motion.

The following example is alternate picked because that happens to be the most economical way to play the line. I've repeated the inside picking motion to allow you to focus on it.

Example 10g:

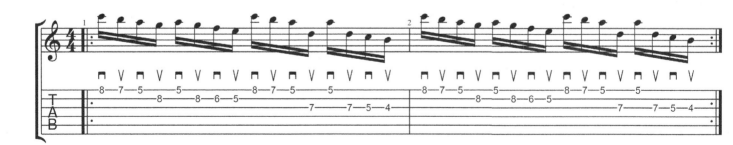

You could say that economy picking is the removal of *outside* picking from your playing. Every time you change strings, you can do it with a direct motion (a sweep) or an inside picked motion.

For example, let's play an E shaped major scale with economy picking. Pay careful attention to the pick strokes – there are no outside picked string crosses here.

Example 10h:

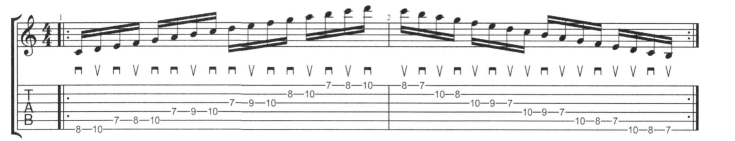

The thing that really helped me get this technique into my subconscious was practicing all of my 7th arpeggios using it. When doing this, you have to really focus on trying to keep everything in time. It's very easy to rush, but we want to avoid that as much as possible.

Example 10i:

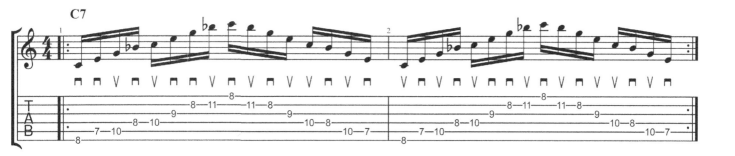

We should practice this in different positions too, like this C shaped arpeggio.

Example 10j:

Here's an ascending arpeggio linked to a descending scale.

Example 10k:

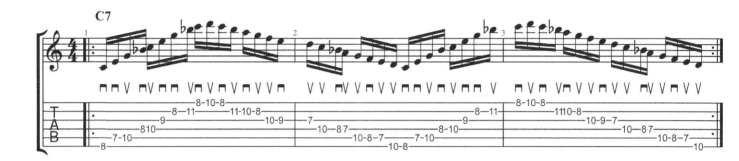

When playing ascending and descending scales, you'll find that the string crossing mechanics change a lot, because there are varying numbers of notes per string. Some players organise their lines to eliminate this issue. Frank Gambale points out that if we want to sweep between strings, we need an odd number of notes per string, then an even number of notes to change direction.

If we organise our scales in three-note-per-string patterns, this facilitates a direct motion between each string change.

Example 10l:

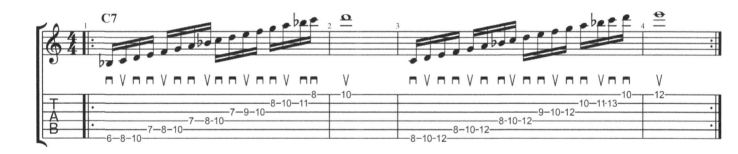

Notice that I wrote the previous example as 1/16th notes. This really pushes us to work on our timing, as the string changes aren't happening on the beats. This is for the best though, because the harder we make our technique practice, the more versatile it'll become in the end. We're not looking to kill ourselves with difficulty here though – you need a Chris Brooks book for that!

Here's the same idea, now applied to a descending scale.

Example 10m:

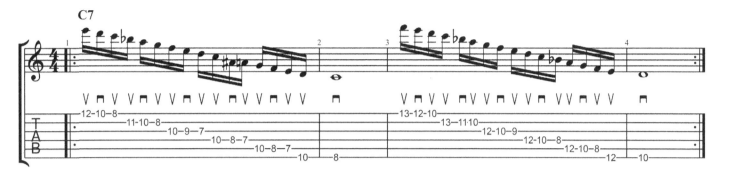

Of course, the exciting thing here is the ability to combine scale patterns with vertical arpeggio ideas. For example, here's an idea based around an Emaj7 chord, arranged with three notes, then one note, on consecutive strings i.e., three notes on the A string, one on the D, three on the G, etc. Odd notes on each string means that we can sweep through them all!

Example 10n:

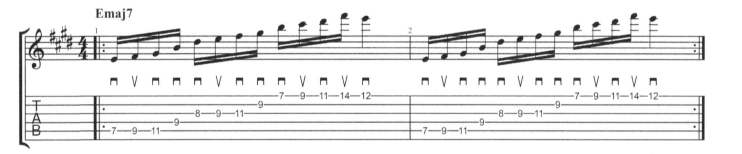

Finally, here's a little adaptation of that idea, now creating an E minor sound that takes us from the 7th fret up to the 15th.

Example 10o:

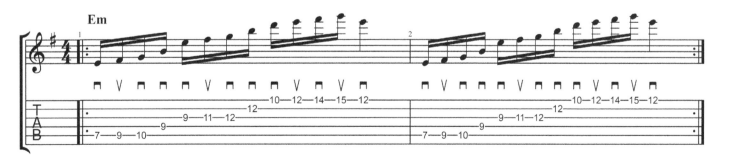

And that's it!

While not comprehensive, we've had a nice workout to get our economy picking happening. Who knows... maybe I'll do a book with 100 little etudes like this one day, but for now, you've got work to do!

Conclusion

And we made it. 10 weeks of practice that mean now, hopefully, you can say you're armed with the skills you need to advance even further in the coming weeks, months and years.

What you choose to do with this information is up to you, but you now have the skills to apply your mind to just about any area of study. The job is never done, but as long as you're getting a little better each day, then you're taking steps in the right direction.

I have plenty of other books you can dig into if you wish, and there will be more practice routine material coming up next year, but don't think that's all there is. There's nothing I enjoy more than taking a chord progression from a jazz standard or pop song, setting up my looper and seeing what I can do with it – so there will be more exploration of chords, arpeggios, scales, and improvisation.

I'll leave you with an alternative idea though.

We've worked extensively on fretboard skills, so you know scales, arpeggios, triads, 7th chords, and much more. You're in a perfect position now to work on some real music theory books. I always found that prior to knowing the fretboard, working from theory books was hard going. When you've got the fretboard down, however, it suddenly becomes much easier to study *how* music works, because you can find it all on the guitar.

I'll reassure you, if you've managed to make it through these 10 weeks (and potentially a full 30 weeks if you've followed the whole series!) then you can do this. You can knuckle down and do anything you set your mind to. Why? Because now you know how to practice.

Keep working, and good luck!

Levi

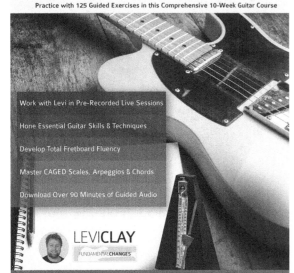

Guided Practice Routines for Guitar – Foundation Level

After a fun yet meaningful warm-up session, Guided Practice Routines for Guitar builds and refines your guitar skills in the following essential areas:

Rhythm – build fretting hand dexterity and excellent alternate picking hand motion. Learn to execute syncopated rhythms and apply them to musical pentatonic scales.

Picking – master picking drills, and use these mechanics on beautiful chord changes.

Drill moveable CAGED shapes – learn to play any chord, arpeggio, or scale in any key with powerful moveable shapes.

Moveable major scales using CAGED – break away from predictable patterns and begin a scale anywhere to 10x your fretboard visualisation.

Advanced picking approaches – learn outside and cross-picking techniques to play more versatile phrases, then combine these with melodies, strumming patterns, and bass notes.

Advanced CAGED exercises – learn the Circle of 4ths with CAGED shapes to play the major scale in every key. Plus combine arpeggios and scales musically.

Legato – develop fluid phrases then combine picking and legato to play any line of music fluently.

Major scale melodic approaches – complete your mastery of the major scale shapes by using sequenced patterns to create unique melodic ideas.

Consolidate your skills – nail a final series of drills that combine everything you've practiced and get even more creative with some sneaky bending tricks.

Guided Practice Routines for Guitar - Intermediate Level

This second volume builds and refines your guitar skills in the following essential areas:

Foundational Techniques Review – review and sharpen the areas of technique that will form the foundation of what's to come.

Closed Voice Triads – learn to visualise CAGED chord shapes and break them into smaller, closed voice triads. Quickly 4x your chord voicing options.

Dominating Dominant 7s – get fluent with one of the most important chord and scale sounds in Blues, Rock, Country and Jazz.

Playing 1/8th and 1/16th Note Rhythms – sort out your rhythm skills once and for all with Levi's no-nonsense approach.

Major 7 and Minor 7 workout – a complete workout for major 7 and minor 7 chords. You'll cover multiple chord voicings and scales all over the neck. Then you'll use these to play some must-know song progressions.

Mastering Intervals – break out of clichéd patterns and runs by creating sequenced patterns using 3rds, 4ths, 5ths, 6ths and 7th intervals.

Embellishing CAGED Chord Voicings – this vital routine teaches how to connect closed voice triads across the fretboard, from position to position, adding musical embellishments.

Articulation and Phrasing – learn one of the most important articulation techniques in modern guitar, and effortlessly combine alternate picking with legato.

Drilling Minor Modal Scales – dive into the Dorian minor scale – an essential tool in your soloing arsenal.

38116622R00057